THE SIMPLE ART OF
NAPKIN FOLDING

THE SIMPLE ART OF
NAPKIN FOLDING

*94 Fancy Folds for Every
Tabletop Occasion*

Linda Hetzer
Illustrated by Robert Penny

Hearst Books
New York

ACKNOWLEDGMENTS

I would like to thank Allen Bragdon for believing in the book, and Helen J. Anderson, Marilyn Hayden, Ruth Hetzer, Christine Siss, Jean Skidmore, Gail Yano, and Hortense Zeh Yost for contributing their talents. A special thanks to Michael Ginsburg for his love and support.

Copyright © 1980 by The Hearst Corporation

Previously published in 1980 as *Fancy Folds*

Recognizing the importance of preserving what has been written, it is the policy of William Morrow and Company, Inc., and its imprints and affiliates to have the books it publishes printed on acid-free paper, and we exert our best efforts to that end.

Library of Congress Cataloging in Publication Data

Hetzer, Linda

The Simple Art of Napkin Folding.

Includes index.

1. Napkin folding. I. Penny, Robert. II. Title.

TX879.H47   642'.7   80-19884
ISBN 0-688-10280-8

1 2 3 4 5 6 7 8 9 10

Printed in U.S.A.

Table of Contents

Serviettes

"The serviettes or table napkins should be neatly and tastefully folded when first put on the table. In ordinary family use they are often folded smoothly and slipped through napkin rings made of silver, ivory or bone; in fact, after the first use this is usually done, each member of the family having his own marked ring. In the following pages we give instructions and illustrations showing many ways of making these useful articles an ornament to the table, but these fancy designs are not fashionable in the household now, and the serviette should simply be folded neatly and laid flat on the plate.

The accompanying engravings depict the designs most in favour and the methods of folding them. It must, however, be remembered that it is useless to attempt anything but the most simple forms unless the napkins have been slightly starched and smoothly ironed. In every case the folding must be exact, or the result will be slovenly and unsightly.

The usual size of these indispensable accompaniments to the dinner table is a square measuring about 30 inches. The designs in the following pages are worked out with a square serviette, and there is a diagram showing how each fold is made and the effect that is produced in every case.

A small dinner roll or a piece of bread cut thick, about 3 inches square, should be placed in each napkin, when such designs as 'The Boar's Head,' 'The Mitre,' or 'The Bishop,' are used, and the appearance of the dinner-table may be greatly improved by putting a flower or small bouquet in napkins folded into patterns like 'The Vase' and 'The Rose.'"

From *Mrs. Beeton's Book of Household Management,* 1909

6

Introduction

Any meal may be transformed into a celebration when dressed up with fancifully folded napkins. This delightful touch is one of the easiest and least expensive ways of creating an attractive table because almost any napkin—even paper—will do for most of the folds. What makes napkin folding so intriguing is the great variety of shapes that can be created for all sorts of different effects. Fans, crowns, and swans, for example, are elegant, pyramids are casual, artichokes are lovely as well as practical, and animal faces and airplanes are just plain fun.

More than three centuries ago, napkin folding was developed into an art, but the practice has drifted in and out of favor following the vicissitudes of table-setting style. The illustration below, taken from a 1639 Italian book on meat carving and other entertaining arts, demonstrates the incredible intricacy with which stiffly starched napkins were once turned into such elaborate shapes as rigged sailing ships and turreted fortresses. Intricate folds like those are rarely, if ever, seen today, but even less ornate forms can cause a sensation at a dinner party. Try some or all of the folds illustrated on the following pages and see what a welcome reception they will get from your family and friends. You will soon discover how one fold leads to another, even to one of your own creation.

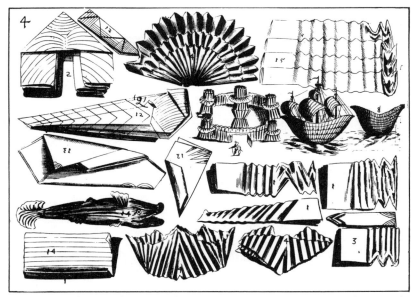

From *Litretrattati di messr* . . . by Mattia Geigher. Padua, Italy, 1639. Courtesy of the Rare Book Division, The New York Public Library, Astor, Lenox and Tilden Foundations.

Creative Suggestions

Fancifully folded napkins, no matter how simply done, improve the look of any table, whether the occasion is formal or a family meal.

A beautifully folded napkin may become a foil for a place card. The card may be set on top of a napkin or tucked into one of the folds. The Cathedral, Diamond, Double Bill, Fortunella, Philodendron, Reflections or Wedding Ring folds are among those that are suitable for place cards.

Certain folds that will comfortably enclose a small favor or flower blossom are particularly charming on a table. Good folds to use for this purpose are the Algonquin, Erin, Flower Basket, New Square, Phoenix, and Pyramid.

Other napkin folds are grand enough to make a novel centerpiece. Try setting a bowl of fruit between two Preening Peacocks, or place a Swan next to a bowl that holds a solitary floating blossom, or line up a row of Birds-of-Paradise down the center of a table.

A combination of folds can also be very attractive on a table. When entertaining eight or more people, choose two different napkin shapes and alternate them at your place settings. You might combine the Candle with the Mexican Fan, the Party Hat with the Party Wheel, the Peony with the Palm Frond, or the Fleur-de-lis with the Hyacinth. Experiment to find your own favorite combinations.

Children take delight in napkins of different shapes, and some of those in the Children's Party section make wonderful favors. For example, write each child's name on a Royal Crown and let it serve as a party hat. Or, for very young children, make Pinwheels with small squares of colored paper (such as Origami paper) and attach them to straws. Children have fun making such favors themselves. Supply them with napkins and crayons so they can create a menagerie of Animal Faces or a squadron of Paper Airplanes.

Napkin folds that accommodate silverware are used to best advantage at a buffet or picnic

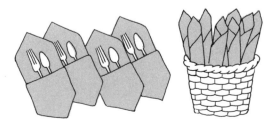

where convenience is essential. Not only do they enhance the look of a table but they provide the easiest way for a guest to pick up both napkin and cutlery at the same time. Such folds can be arranged in patterns on a buffet table to make them even more appealing. Try overlapping flat folds such as the Regimental Stripe, Philodendron, or Buffet Servers in a long row or fan them out to form a circle. If space is at a premium, set standing shapes such as the Erin, Candle, or Palm Frond in a basket, flower pot, or vase.

Exciting table settings often depend as much on a variety of color and pattern as on anything

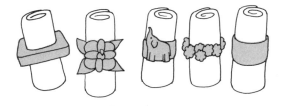

else. It is more interesting to vary napkin folds from meal to meal and party to party than to use the same favorite fold all the time. Also try using different napkins—a floral print, a stripe, or a plaid—in addition to plain ones. Try place mats and coordinated napkins rather than a formal tablecloth for a change, and

experiment with all kinds of napkin rings—silver, wood, plastic, or intertwined flowers. Instead of a floral bouquet, set a bowl of fruit or an arrangement of fresh vegetables at the center of the table. The wide range of possible variations is what makes table setting so challenging and so much fun.

Although fancy napkin folds will enhance any table setting, every fold in this book is not suitable for every table or every napkin. Test the folds you like with the napkins you have to make sure they are complementary in terms of size and pattern. Even if your napkins look wonderful in a particular fold, it may not work in every table setting, depending on the amount of silverware and china, and the size of the centerpiece. Also, make sure the napkin fold is in keeping with the occasion. Obviously, the table setting for a Christmas dinner should look different from a backyard picnic.

Napkin Placement

Traditionally, napkins have been placed either to the left of the forks or at the center of the plate, and, usually, they have been folded into a rectangle for dinner or a triangle for luncheon. But now that we are living in more casual times, you can throw tradition to the winds with beautifully folded napkins placed wherever they look best to you. Depending on the shape you chose, the napkin can be set at the center of the plate, in a glass, above the plate, or even to the right of the spoons (a favorite place for napkins around the turn of the century). For a completely different look, place a napkin with an elongated fold between the plate and the edge of the table, or tuck a flat folded napkin between two plates in a formal place setting. At a seated dinner where guests will serve themselves from a buffet, use an elaborate shape to fill the place of the dinner plate before the guests are seated.

Whatever fold you choose, try it in several positions to see which looks best. Suggestions for placing a variety of folds are illustrated on the opposite page.

A traditional dinner fold is a rectangular shape, placed with the open edge next to the forks so the napkin can be lifted and opened most easily and with the least amount of movement.

A traditional luncheon fold is a triangle placed with the folded edge next to the fork and the point facing out.

Traditional Dinner Fold

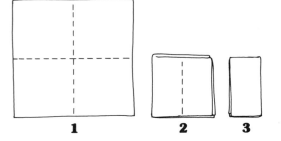

1. *Fold the napkin in quarters.*
2. *Then fold it in half to form a rectangle.*
3. *Place the open edges next to the fork.*

Traditional Luncheon Fold

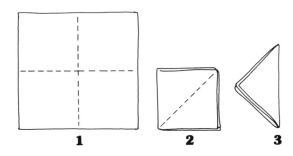

1. *Fold the napkin in quarters.*
2. *Then fold it in half diagonally to form a triangle.*
3. *Place the folded edge next to the fork.*

Left of the forks: Any fold that is not set in a glass is appropriate here. Irish Ripples is shown above.

Center of the plate: A full fold, such as Party Wheel (above), Fleur-de-lis, or Artichoke looks good on a plate.

Above the plate: Folds with a strong silhouette such as the Bird-of-Paradise (above) or Mexican Fan are suitable.

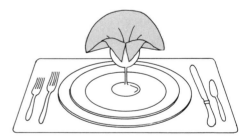

Below the plate: For an unusual look, place a long fold like the Bow Tie (above) or Roll below the plate.

Right of the plate: For a change of pace, set Bishop's Hat (above) or other upright shape next to the spoons.

In a glass: For a festive look, place the Poinsettia (above), Soave, Peacock, or Temple Bells in a glass.

Between two plates: For a formal dinner, slip a flat fold like the Luncheon (above) between two dishes.

Without a plate: For a seated buffet, place a full fold like Nosegay (above) at the center of the place setting.

Table Settings

Guidelines for setting a table are most helpful if they are regarded as just that, not as rigid rules. Basically, a table should be set to suit the needs of the menu you are serving and your own table accessories.

Following are some general guidelines for setting a table. Silverware should be placed one inch from the edge of a table or place mat; place mats are set one inch from the edge of the table. Flatware is arranged in order of use, starting at the outside and working toward the plate. For formal meals, dessert silver can be placed on the table, but on other occasions it is usually brought in with dessert.

A coffee cup and saucer are never part of a place setting, except at breakfast. Coffee is served separately, at which time a spoon may be placed on the saucer.

The water glass should be set above the knife, to the right of the plate. The wine glass or glasses are then arranged to the right of the water glass in order of service.

Bread-and-butter plates are generally not used in a formal dinner, but for an informal occasion they are placed to the left of the plate above the forks. The butter knife rests on the plate, with the blade in, either parallel to the forks or perpendicular to them across the top of the plate and the handle to the right.

When the salad plate is part of a table setting, it is placed above and slightly to the left of the forks. It is also proper to serve the salad as a separate course and to bring in salad plates at the appropriate time.

When setting the table, allow at least 18 inches for each place setting. Crowding a place setting into less space will not allow diners enough room to eat.

When choosing a centerpiece, remember to keep it low enough so guests can easily see over it and small enough so it will not encroach on the place settings.

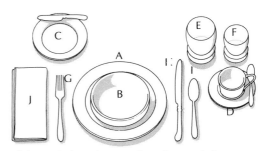

Breakfast: A luncheon plate is used for eggs or any other main course. The cereal bowl goes on the luncheon plate. Only at breakfast is it good form to have the cup and saucer on the table at the beginning of the meal.

A Luncheon plate	E Water glass
B Cereal bowl	F Juice glass
C Bread-and-butter plate	G Fork
with butter knife	H Knife
D Cup and saucer with	I Teaspoon
teaspoon	J Napkin

Luncheon: The plate for a first course, if any, is placed on top of the luncheon plate. To serve soup, set the soup bowl and a liner plate on top of the luncheon plate and have a soup spoon already in place at the right of the teaspoon. A fork for the first course would be placed to the left of the luncheon fork. Salad can be served with the main course on the luncheon plate.

A Luncheon plate	E Wine glass
B Soup bowl (or other	F Luncheon fork
first course plate) on a	G Knife
liner plate	H Teaspoon
C Bread-and-butter plate	I Soup spoon
with butter knife	J Napkin
D Water glass	

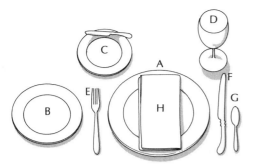

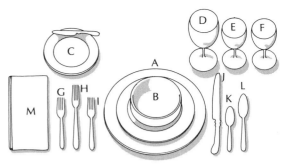

Family dinner: If there is no first course, the napkin is usually placed at the center of the dinner plate. The salad plate is then set to the left of the forks. The teaspoon in the place setting is used for dessert or a dessert fork is carried in with that course.

A Dinner plate
B Salad plate
C Bread-and-butter plate with butter knife
D Water glass
E Fork
F Knife
G Teaspoon
H napkin

Formal dinner: Utensils for the first course and a service plate on which it is set are part of a formal place setting. When the service plate is removed with the first course dishes, it is replaced with a dinner plate. Silverware for dessert can be set in advance or brought in with that course.

A Service plate
B Soup bowl on a liner plate
C Salad plate
D Water glass
E Wine glass
F Wine glass
G Salad fork
H Dinner fork
I Dessert fork
J Knife
K Teaspoon
L Soup spoon
M Napkin

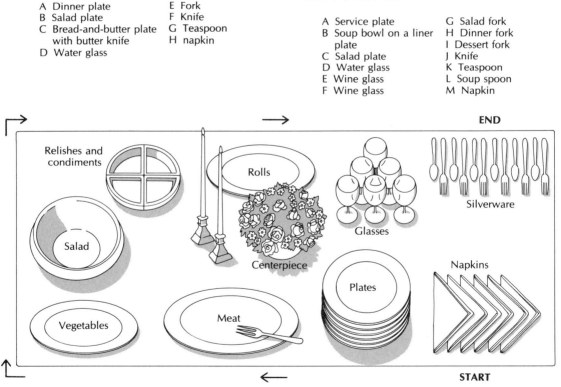

Buffet: A buffet table should be arranged so that guests can serve themselves in the easiest way possible. A logical order is to start with napkins and plates, follow with a variety of foods and end with bread or rolls, a drink, and then the silverware. That way guests will not have to contend with a drink and the utensils while helping themselves to food.

Stain Removal Chart

Stain	Washable fabrics	Dryclean fabrics
Alcoholic beverages, soft drinks, wine	On a fresh stain, sponge with cold water. On a stain that has dried, soak in cold water. Then wash in warm water using soap or detergent.	On a fresh stain, sprinkle immediately with cornstarch until the liquid is absorbed. On a dry stain, sponge with cold water.
Ballpoint pen	Place paper towels under the napkin and sponge with denatured alcohol. Each time you apply more alcohol, move the stain to a clean part of the paper towels. Then launder using bleach if the napkin is white.	At the dry cleaner's specify that the stain was made by a ballpoint pen.
Berries and other fruits, fruit juices	Sprinkle immediately with salt to absorb the liquid. Apply white vinegar to the stain before laundering.	Follow the instructions for washable fabrics but after treating the stain, send the napkin to the dry cleaner's.
Candle wax	Rub wax with an ice cube until hard, then scrape off with a blunt knife. Or, place paper towels under and over the napkin and press with a warm iron. Change the paper towels frequently until all the wax has been absorbed by the towels.	Follow the instructions for washable fabrics. If after removing the wax, a stain remains rub with cleaning fluid.
Catsup, tomato sauce	Soak in warm water and liquid detergent, then launder using bleach if possible.	At the dry cleaner's, specify that the stain is tomato sauce.
Chewing gum	Rub with an ice cube, then scrape off with a blunt knife.	Follow the instructions for washable fabrics.
Chocolate, coffee, tea	Sponge with cleaning fluid. Let the napkin dry, then launder using bleach if possible.	At the dry cleaner's, specify the source of the stain.

Stain	Washable fabrics	Dryclean fabrics
Ink	Pour water through the napkin until the water runs clear. Then apply detergent and white vinegar. Rinse well.	Follow the instructions for washable fabrics.
Lipstick and other cosmetics	Rub the stain with detergent dissolved in lukewarm water, then launder.	Use a greasy stain solvent, then dry-clean.
Mildew	Launder, then dry in the sunlight.	Dry-clean, then air in the sunlight.
Milk, cream, ice cream, butter	Soak immediately in cold water, then rinse thoroughly. Launder.	Sprinkle immediately with cornstarch. Allow the napkin to dry thoroughly, then brush the powder away.
Mustard	Soak in cold water and detergent or a soaking product. Then launder.	At the dry-cleaner's, specify that the stain is mustard.
Pencil	Erase with a soft eraser. Work detergent into any remaining stain. Then launder.	Erase with a soft eraser, then dry-clean.
Protein such as egg, meat, meat juice, gravy, blood	Soak in cold water. If the stain is still visible, sponge with cleaning fluid. Allow to dry before laundering.	Sponge with cold water; use cleaning fluid if necessary. Dry-clean.
Scorch	Sponge with hydrogen pyroxide or ammonia. Rinse well and launder.	Dampen with hydrogen peroxide until stain is removed.
Vomit	Soak in a salt-water solution (one-quarter cup salt to one quart water). Launder.	Follow the instructions for washable fabrics, then dry-clean.

What You Need to Know Before You Start Folding

Napkins come in a great variety of materials ranging from double damask linen to paper. Among the most popular napkin fabrics are pure cotton, blends of cotton or linen with synthetics, and pure synthetics. Each material is noted for its own special characteristics—linen for elegance, cotton for durability, synthetics for easy care, and paper for practicality—and each responds differently to being folded. Linen napkins will even fold differently depending on the weight and design of the fabric.

Today most napkins come in one of three sizes: 12- or 13-inch-square paper napkins sold in grocery stores; 17-inch-square paper napkins in solids or prints, available at grocery stores or shops that specialize in party fare; 17-inch-square cloth napkins, usually made of a synthetic such as polyester or a cotton-and-polyester blend; and 20-inch-square cloth napkins of cotton, linen, or a blend. Anyone fortunate enough to have inherited grandmother's table linens may have napkins ranging in size from 22 to 30 inches square.

Most of the folds illustrated on the following pages were made with a 20-inch-square cloth napkin. Any variations in size or material are spelled out in the directions. Results may vary from the illustration if deviations are made in napkin size or material.

The index on page 124 indicates the sizes and materials appropriate for each of the folds, however, you can experiment to determine the folds that work best with your napkins.

Directions for all the folds start with a napkin opened to its full size. For most of the shapes, napkins that have previously been folded in quarters do not have to be pressed flat, but, if pressing is necessary, lightly apply spray starch to the napkin. None of the folds illustrated were made with starched napkins, but spray starch will help to eliminate creases, and it adds body to a limp fabric.

Folds that require support in a glass or napkin ring should be tested before a dinner party to make sure they are compatible with your glasses or napkin rings.

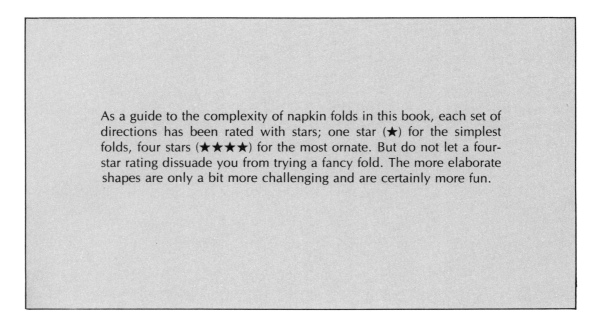

As a guide to the complexity of napkin folds in this book, each set of directions has been rated with stars; one star (★) for the simplest folds, four stars (★★★★) for the most ornate. But do not let a four-star rating dissuade you from trying a fancy fold. The more elaborate shapes are only a bit more challenging and are certainly more fun.

Quick Folds

Astoria

The Astoria will highlight a beautiful monogram or corner design as shown at right. With plain napkins, the fold can be placed with the point in the opposite direction.

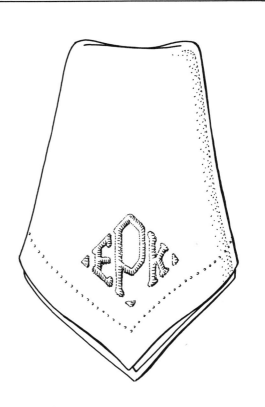

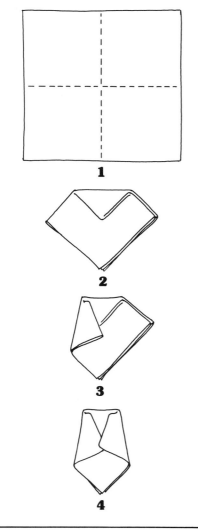

★ Instructions

1. Fold the napkin in quarters.

2. Place the napkin at an angle with the free points at the bottom and the monogram or design, if any, face down. Fold down the top points.

3. Fold the left point just past the center.

4. Fold the right point just past the center and turn the napkin over.

Bow Tie

The Bow Tie is a good fold to use when lunch or dinner is a casual affair. This shape must be folded with a cloth napkin—any size will do—because a paper napkin does not have the strength or resilience to withstand knotting.

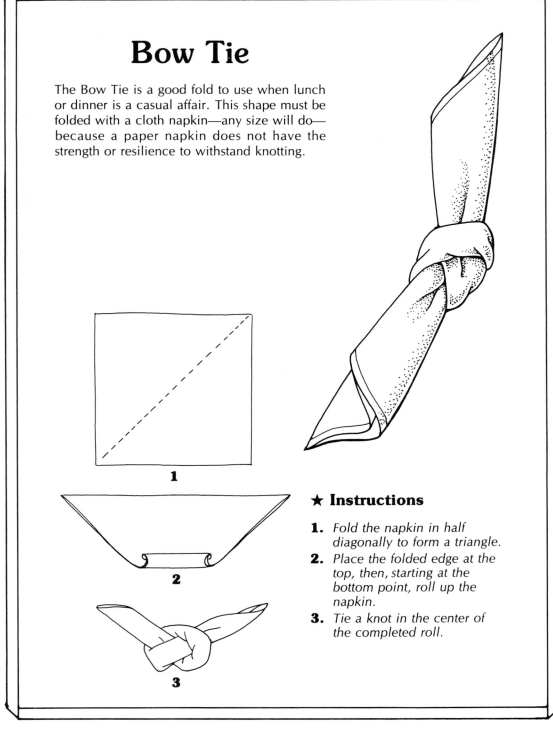

1

2

3

★ Instructions

1. *Fold the napkin in half diagonally to form a triangle.*
2. *Place the folded edge at the top, then, starting at the bottom point, roll up the napkin.*
3. *Tie a knot in the center of the completed roll.*

Chloe

Chloe is a dressy variation of the traditional triangular fold that is suitable for a formal dinner party or a casual weekend brunch. To make this fold, use any size napkin in cloth or paper.

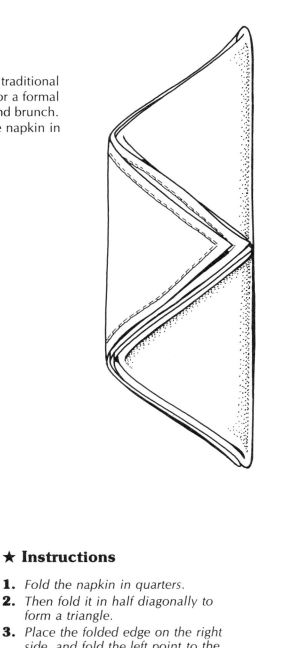

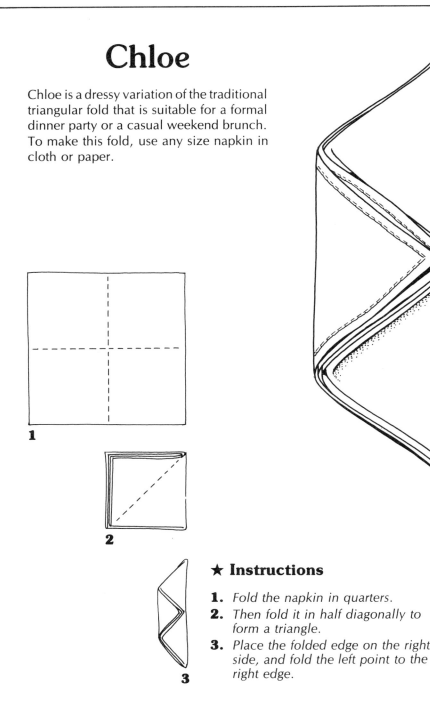

1

2

3

★ Instructions

1. *Fold the napkin in quarters.*
2. *Then fold it in half diagonally to form a triangle.*
3. *Place the folded edge on the right side, and fold the left point to the right edge.*

Debevoise

The Debevoise, an elegant fold, is the perfect size and shape for placement to the left of the forks. The shape is a classic that will harmonize with any table setting from very simple to extremely elaborate.

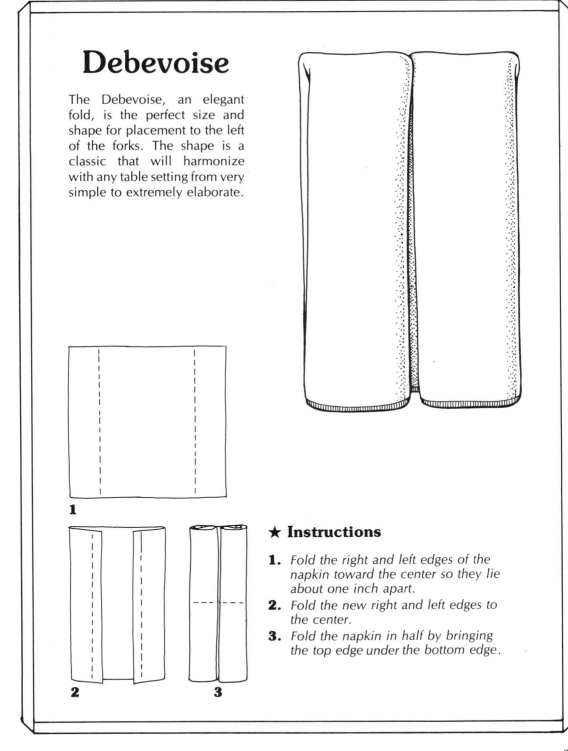

1

2   **3**

★ Instructions

1. *Fold the right and left edges of the napkin toward the center so they lie about one inch apart.*
2. *Fold the new right and left edges to the center.*
3. *Fold the napkin in half by bringing the top edge under the bottom edge.*

Fan

The Fan, a classic fold, can be anchored in a glass of almost any shape. Or, if a small cloth or paper napkin is used, it can be anchored in a sturdy napkin ring.

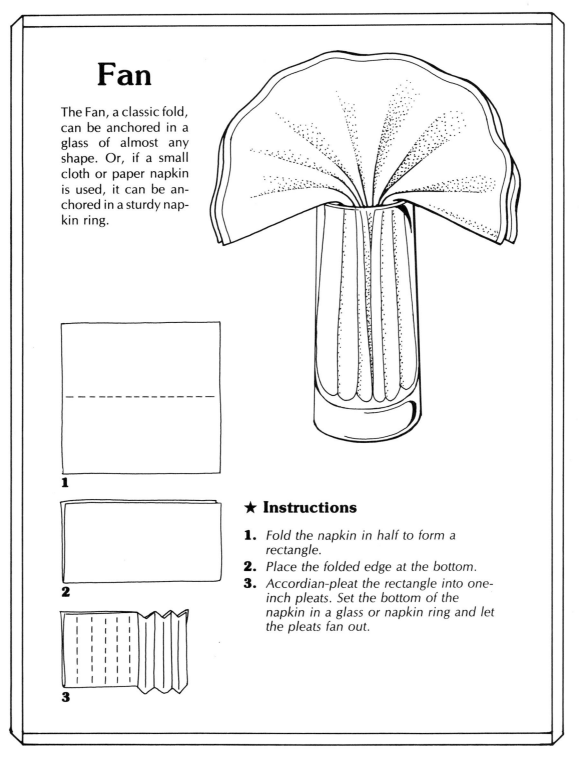

1

2

3

★ Instructions

1. *Fold the napkin in half to form a rectangle.*

2. *Place the folded edge at the bottom.*

3. *Accordian-pleat the rectangle into one-inch pleats. Set the bottom of the napkin in a glass or napkin ring and let the pleats fan out.*

Luncheon

The Luncheon is a simple fold, which, as its name applies, is particularly appropriate for a luncheon. It can be placed with the corners pointing up, as shown, or with the corners pointing down. The fold can also be used with or without a napkin ring. To make the clover-blossom napkin ring in the drawing see page 123.

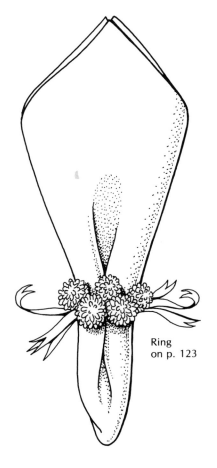

Ring
on p. 123

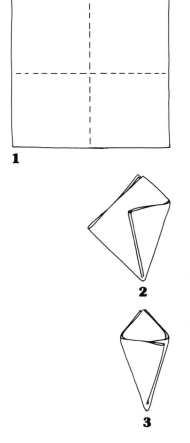

1

2

3

★ Instructions

1. *Fold the napkin in quarters.*
2. *Place the napkin so the free points are on top and fold the lower right edge over the center, as shown.*
3. *Fold the lower left edge to the right side. Turn the napkin over and slip the bottom three or four inches through a napkin ring.*

Nosegay

The Nosegay is a charming shape to use for any casual lunch or dinner. A simple or elaborate napkin ring can be used. To make the flower-blossom napkin ring in the drawing, see page 123.

Flower Napkin Ring on p. 123

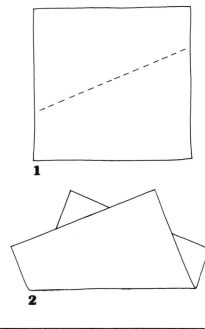

1

2

★ Instructions

1. *Fold the napkin in half diagonally but slightly off center so the two top points are the same height.*

2. *Place the folded edge at the bottom. Hold the napkin in the center of this edge as you pull about three inches of it through a napkin ring.*

Pierre

The Pierre is stately enough to use at even the most formal dinner parties. Because the center band is formed by folding over the reverse side of the napkin, the fabric should be reversible, or at least look the same on both sides.

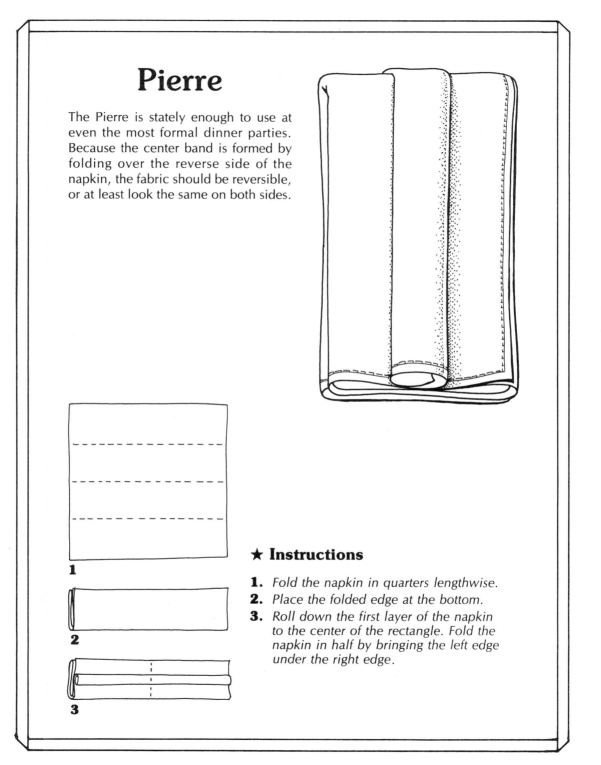

1

2

3

★ Instructions

1. *Fold the napkin in quarters lengthwise.*

2. *Place the folded edge at the bottom.*

3. *Roll down the first layer of the napkin to the center of the rectangle. Fold the napkin in half by bringing the left edge under the right edge.*

Roll

The Roll, perhaps the simplest of all the folds, can be made with any napkin, regardless of its size, weight, color, or pattern. Quick to make, this fold can be placed vertically or horizontally next to the forks, in the center of the plate, or above the plate. To make a fabric-covered napkin ring that coordinates with your place setting see page 122.

Fabric Napkin
Ring on p. 122

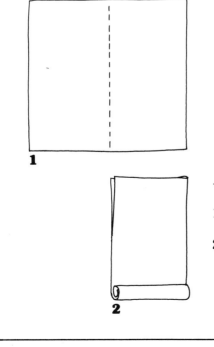

1

★ Instructions

1. *Fold the napkin in half to form a rectangle.*
2. *Starting at a narrow end, roll up the napkin and slip it through a napkin ring.*

2

Soave

This casual shape can be folded with brightly colored napkins or with ones that have a striking design such as checks, plaids, florals or bandanna prints. For a variation on the fold, turn down one of the ends.

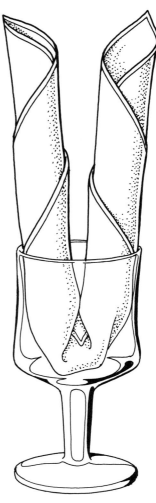

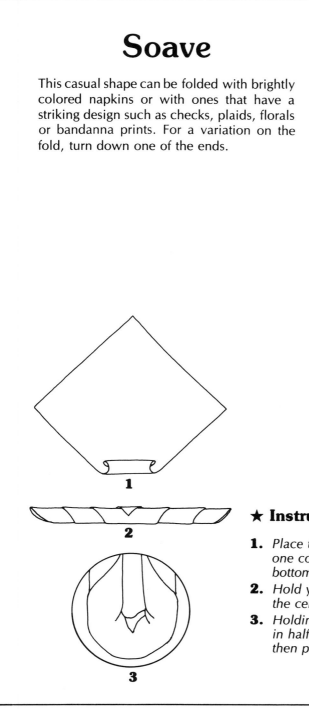

★ Instructions

1. *Place the napkin flat on the table with one corner facing you. Starting at the bottom corner, roll up the napkin.*

2. *Hold your finger on the corner in the center of the completed roll.*

3. *Holding this end in place, fold the tube in half to catch the end securely and then place the tube in a glass.*

Sphinx

The sphinx is a very simple fold to make, and the napkin stands without the need of starch. The fold looks good to the left of the forks or in the center of the plate.

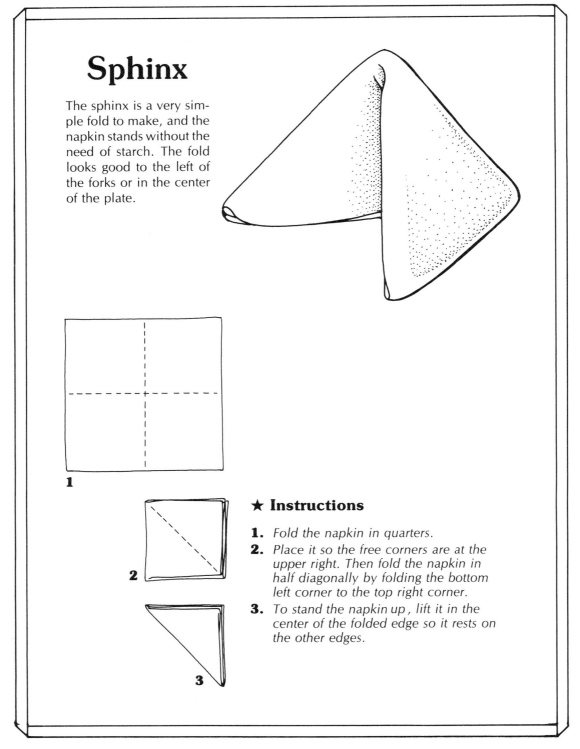

1

2

3

★ Instructions

1. *Fold the napkin in quarters.*
2. *Place it so the free corners are at the upper right. Then fold the napkin in half diagonally by folding the bottom left corner to the top right corner.*
3. *To stand the napkin up, lift it in the center of the folded edge so it rests on the other edges.*

Fancy Folds

Ahoy

The Ahoy is a simple but graceful fold that requires a 17- to 20-inch cloth napkin. The fold can stand on the plate, above the plate, to the left of the forks, or above the forks. For a variation on the fold, tuck the two ends into each other and place the napkin so the point is facing the diner.

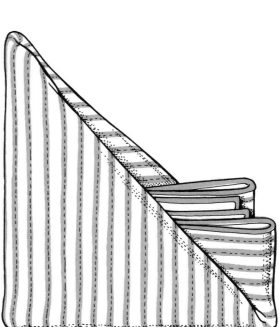

Variation

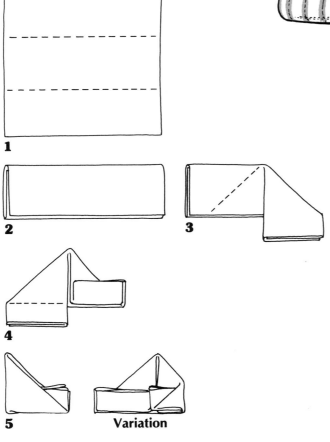

★★ Instructions

1. Fold the napkin in thirds.
2. Place the napkin so the folded edge is at the top.
3. Place your finger at the center of the top edge and fold down the right side. Then fold down the left side.
4. Fold the bottom edges up so they are even with the layer beneath.
5. Fold the napkin in half and stand it up.

Variation: After step 4, fold the napkin in thirds and tuck the right side into the left side. Stand the napkin up.

Algonquin

The Algonquin looks especially elegant when folded with a 20-inch-square linen napkin. For a variation on the fold, opposite corners of the napkin may be folded under. Either way, the bands lend themselves to a number of treatments. They can accommodate a single flower, as shown in the drawing at right, a place card, or a small party favor can be snuggled inside the bands. If you tuck in a flower or place card, place the napkin in the center of the plate. The fold, without a favor, can be placed to the left of the forks.

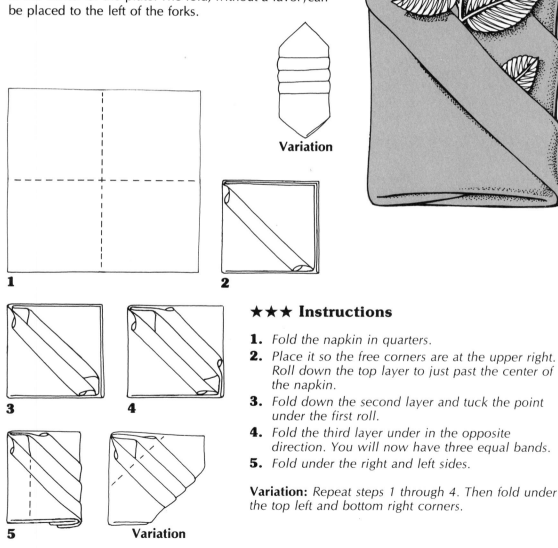

Variation

1

2

3

4

5

Variation

★★★ Instructions

1. *Fold the napkin in quarters.*

2. *Place it so the free corners are at the upper right. Roll down the top layer to just past the center of the napkin.*

3. *Fold down the second layer and tuck the point under the first roll.*

4. *Fold the third layer under in the opposite direction. You will now have three equal bands.*

5. *Fold under the right and left sides.*

Variation: *Repeat steps 1 through 4. Then fold under the top left and bottom right corners.*

Arrowhead

A turn-of-the-century book on household management suggested that each tablecloth be complemented by two dozen napkins. Napkins of that day came in three sizes: breakfast, 17 to 22 inches; luncheon, 23 to 27 inches; and formal dinner, 29 to 31 inches. By 1921, the recommended size for dinner napkins was 24 to 28 inches and for luncheon 13 to 17 inches—somewhat smaller than those of twenty years earlier but still larger than the average today. For the Arrowhead, either a 17- or 20-inch napkin is suitable.

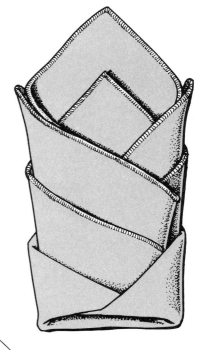

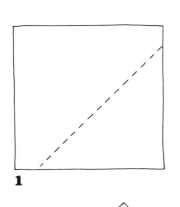

1

2

3

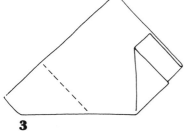

4

5

6

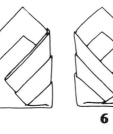

★★★ Instructions

1. *Fold up one corner of the napkin to within about two inches of the opposite corner.*

2. *Place the napkin so the fold is along the bottom edge.*

3. *Turn the napkin over. Place your fingers about two inches apart in the center of the bottom edge. Fold up the sides so right and left portions of the bottom edge are perpendicular to the edge you are holding.*

4. *Fold up the bottom edge.*

5. *Turn the napkin over. Fold over the right side and then the left side.*

6. *Tuck the edge of the left side into the right side. To make the napkin stand up, put your hand down into the center to round out the shape.*

Artichoke

At the turn of the century, the custom at prestigious New York hotels like the Astor and the Delmonico was to fold the napkin into a three-cornered tent shape and place a dinner roll inside. The Artichoke provides an even fancier way to present dinner rolls.

1

2

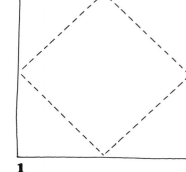

3 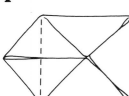   **4**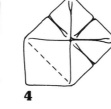

5 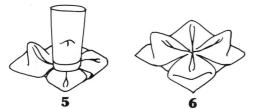   **6**

★★★★ Instructions

1. Fold the corners of the napkin to the center.
2. The napkin will look like this when all but the last corner are folded in.
3. Now bring the new corners to the center.
4. Turn the napkin over and fold the corners to the center.
5. Place a glass in the center of the napkin to anchor it. Hold it firmly with one hand as you pull out each of the corners from the underside.
6. Give each corner a slight tug to make it stand up.

Astarte

This intricate fold was included in Mrs. Beeton's *Household Management*, published in the middle of the nineteenth century. Still attractive today, it requires a crisp cloth napkin at least 20 inches square.

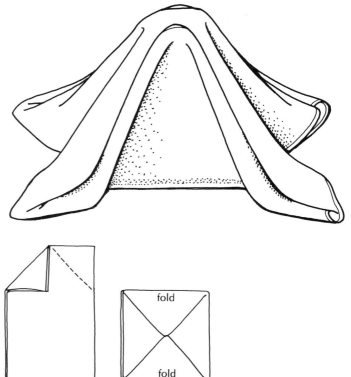

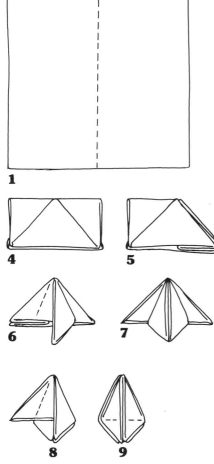

★★★★ Instructions

1. *Fold the napkin in half.*
2. *Fold in each of the corners.*
3. *Fold top and bottom points to the center.*
4. *Fold in half keeping triangles on the outside.*
5. *Holding napkin at the center top point, tuck the upper right corner inside the napkin so it lies in the center of the bottom edge. Repeat with the upper left corner.*
6. *Bring top layer of the right edge to the center.*
7. *Bring top layer of the left edge to the center.*
8. *Turn napkin over. Bring right edge to the center.*
9. *Bring left edge to the center. Stand the napkin up, placing the bottom points flat on the table so they form four supporting legs. Allow the napkin to open slightly. Illustration above shows front or back view of the folded shape.*

Bird-of-Paradise

The Bird-of-Paradise is an intricate fold that requires a cloth napkin at least 20 inches square. The napkin should be of medium weight so the petals will stand up, but not too thick or the base will become too bulky.

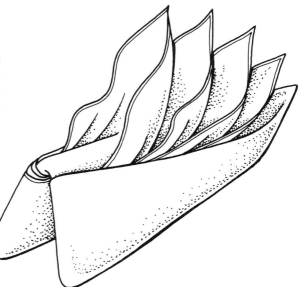

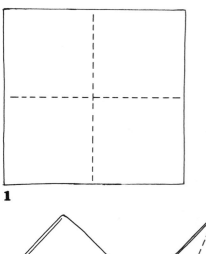

1

2

3

4

5

6

★★★★ Instructions

1. *Fold the napkin in quarters.*
2. *Place it so the free corners are at the bottom, then fold it in half diagonally to form a triangle with the free corners on top.*
3. *Hold your finger on the top corner as you fold first the right side, then the left side, to the center.*
4. *Fold the lower points under the napkin.*
5. *Fold the triangle in half by bringing the left side under the right side. The center fold will open slightly.*
6. *Lay the napkin down so the corner points are on top. Holding the broad end of the napkin with one hand, pull up the four corner points to form petals.*

Bishop's Hat

The Bishop's Hat is a traditional fold that has graced tables all over the world. With the front sides of the hat pulled down, the shape can be made to resemble a Butterfly, and with the sides pulled down and tucked into the fold, it looks like a Blossom.

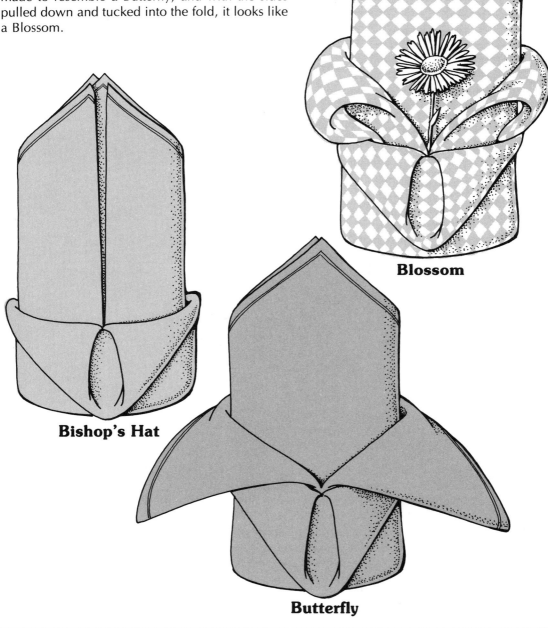

Blossom

Bishop's Hat

Butterfly

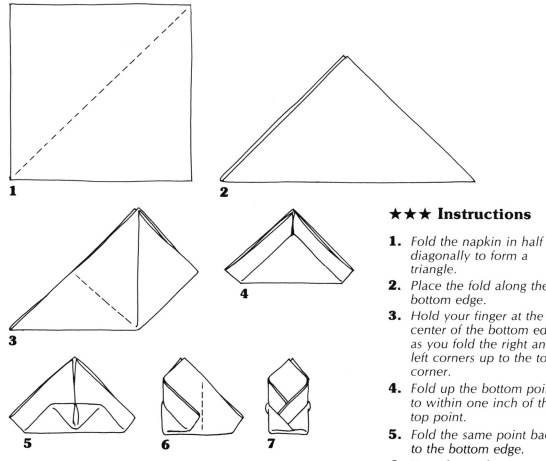

★★★ Instructions

1. Fold the napkin in half diagonally to form a triangle.

2. Place the fold along the bottom edge.

3. Hold your finger at the center of the bottom edge as you fold the right and left corners up to the top corner.

4. Fold up the bottom point to within one inch of the top point.

5. Fold the same point back to the bottom edge.

6. Turn the napkin over and fold the left side toward the center.

7. Fold the right side over the left side, tucking the point into the left fold. Stand the napkin up.

Butterfly Variation

Butterfly variation: *Pull down the left and right sides of the Bishop's Hat until they are horizontal.*

Blossom Variation

Blossom variation: *Turn down the right and left sides and tuck the points into the fold.*

Buffet Servers

A buffet is a wonderfully convivial way to serve a meal. It allows guests more choice in food and gives them a chance to converse with many people. When giving a buffet, always try to make it as uncomplicated as possible for the guests. One way to do that is to have the silverware and napkins together in a convenient package. Here are two different styles of Buffet Servers from which to choose.

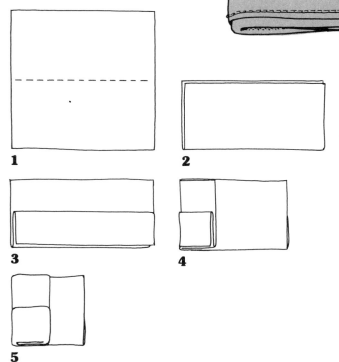

Buffet Server I

★ Instructions

1. *Fold the napkin in half to form a rectangle.*
2. *Place it so the folded edge is at the bottom.*
3. *Bring the top edge of the first layer to the bottom edge.*
4. *Turn the napkin over. Bring the left edge to the center.*
5. *Fold this section over on itself two more times in the same direction.*

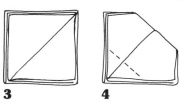

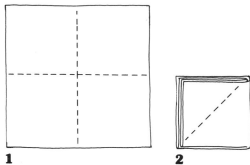

Buffet Server II

★ Instructions

1. Fold the napkin in quarters.

2. Place the napkin so the free points are at the upper left.

3. Fold the upper left corner of the top layer down to the lower right corner.

4. Fold under the top right and bottom left corners.

Candle

The Candle, a simple shape that looks appropriate with modern china and glassware, is a popular fold in Swedish and Danish table settings.

This versatile fold can be placed in the center of the plate, to the left of the forks, above the forks, or centered above the plate. For a buffet, a group of napkins folded into Candles makes a nice sculptural addition to the table.

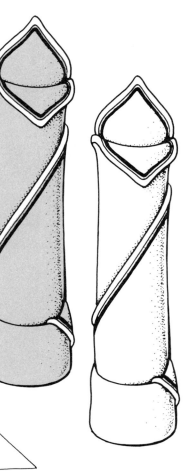

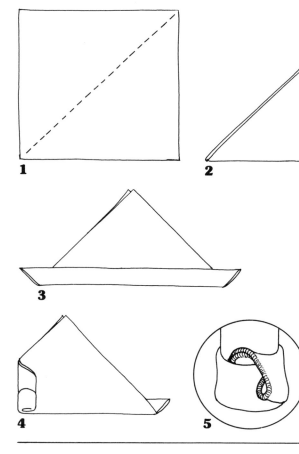

★★ Instructions

1. Fold the napkin in half diagonally to form a triangle.

2. Place the napkin so the fold is along the bottom edge.

3. Fold up the bottom edge about one and one-half inches.

4. Turn the napkin over and roll it up fairly tightly.

5. Stand the candle up and tuck the corner into the cuff to hold the rolled shape in place. If you like, fold down one layer at the tip of the candle to resemble a flickering flame.

Cathedral

The Cathedral looks equally as good in a casual cotton napkin as it does in a fine linen one. Linen for tablecloths and napkins is made from the flax plant, which, according to the earliest records in Europe, was first cultivated in Ireland. The most famous linen was made in Reims, France, until the Hundred Years' War, which ended in 1443, totally destroyed its linen weaving industry. Flanders then became the center of the linen weaving trade.

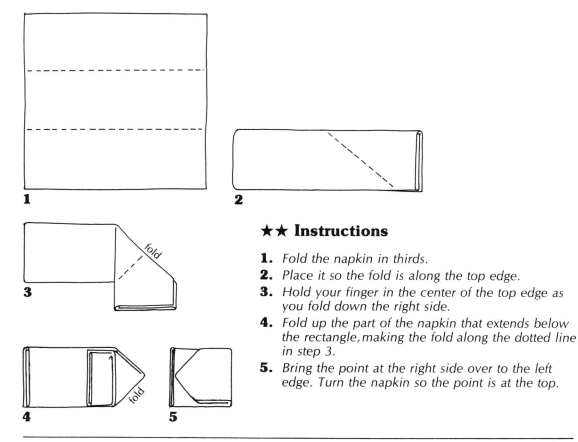

★★ Instructions

1. Fold the napkin in thirds.

2. Place it so the fold is along the top edge.

3. Hold your finger in the center of the top edge as you fold down the right side.

4. Fold up the part of the napkin that extends below the rectangle, making the fold along the dotted line in step 3.

5. Bring the point at the right side over to the left edge. Turn the napkin so the point is at the top.

Crown

The Crown is a traditional fold that has enhanced table settings for years. When standing at each place setting it looks positively regal. The shape is easy to make and can be folded in a variety of fabrics.

Linen fabric for tablecloths and napkins can be damask, which has a design woven in, or oyster linen, which is a plain woven fabric made in many colors and prints.

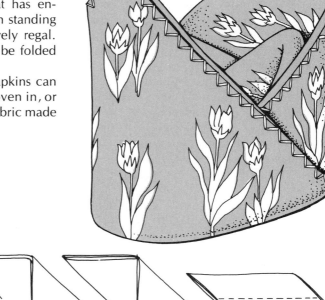

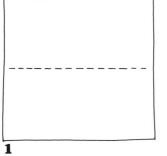

1

2   3   4

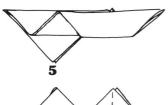

5

6

7

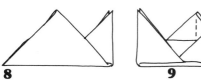

8   9

★★★ Instructions

1. *Fold the napkin in half to make a rectangle.*
2. *Fold the top right corner down to the bottom edge.*
3. *Fold the bottom left corner up to the top edge.*
4. *Turn the napkin over.*
5. *Fold the bottom edge up to the top edge; one triangle will extend below the bottom edge.*
6. *Hold the napkin along the top edge as you turn it over. A second triangle will fall free so there will now be two triangles along the top edge.*
7. *Fold the right quarter of the napkin toward the center, tucking the point under the long fold.*
8. *The napkin will look like this.*
9. *Turn the napkin over. On this side, fold the right quarter toward the center and tuck in the point. Stand the napkin up.*

Davallia

The Davallia, a simple but elegant fold, is particularly versatile. For napkins with a monogram or initial, the fold shown at the right will work best. If the napkins are plain, they can be placed in the opposite direction with the corners pointing up. For a third variation, the narrow end of the napkin can be slipped into a napkin ring. For instructions on embroidering initials on a napkin, see page 118.

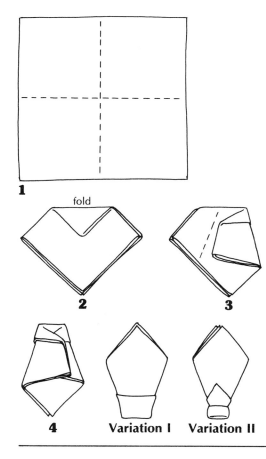

★ Instructions

1. *Fold the napkin in quarters.*

2. *Place the napkin at an angle so the free corners are at the bottom. Fold the top corner to within about four inches of the bottom corner.*

3. *Turn the napkin over and fold the right side diagonally across the center.*

4. *Fold the left side over the right side. Turn the napkin over.*

Variation I: *Turn the napkin so the free corners are pointing up. Tuck the bottom point under.*

Variation II: *Slip the narrow end of the fold in a napkin ring.*

Diamond

The Diamond, a fairly intricate fold that was popular in England at the turn of the century, requires a 20-inch-square cloth napkin. Even when folded with such a large napkin, the completed shape is rather small and fits nicely in any setting. For a variation, turn the Diamond over so the two rolled edges are on top.

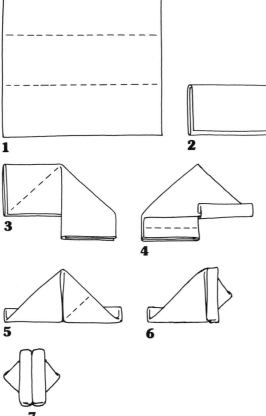

1

2

3

4

5

6

7

★★★★ Instructions

1. *Fold the napkin in thirds.*

2. *Place it so the fold is along the top edge.*

3. *Hold your finger at the center of the top edge as you fold down the right and left sides.*

4. *Turn the napkin over. Then turn up the bottom right edge by making two equal folds. Repeat with the bottom left edge.*

5. *Holding the bottom folds in place, turn the napkin over.*

6. *Fold the bottom right edge up to the center.*

7. *Fold the bottom left edge up to the center. Leave the rolled side up or turn the napkin over for a diamond effect.*

Double Bill

An 1895 catalog from Harrod's, London's quintessential department store, lists three sizes of linen damask napkins: breakfast, 20 to 22 inches; dinner 24 to 27 inches; and extra size, 30 to 32 inches. The catalog also featured figured damask tableclothes and napkins in "eighteenth century style," specially designed for Harrod's. The Double Bill would have been as suitable in 1895 as it is today.

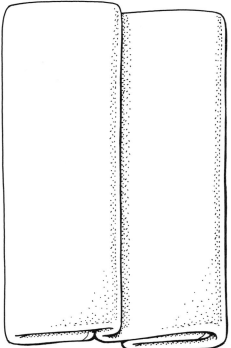

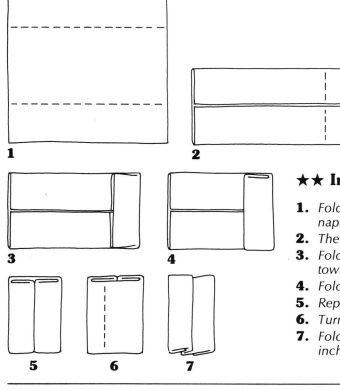

1 **2**

3 **4**

5 **6** **7**

★★ Instructions

1. *Fold the top and bottom edges of the napkin to the center.*

2. *The napkin will look like this.*

3. *Fold the right edge about two inches toward the center.*

4. *Fold the new right edge to the center.*

5. *Repeat steps 3 and 4 with the left side.*

6. *Turn the napkin over.*

7. *Fold the left edge over to within two inches of the right edge.*

Echeverria

The word damask, which has come to mean figured linen, comes from the French word *damasse* used to describe a type of metal decoration.

In the Middle Ages, gallant warriors embellished their swords with patterns of curved grooves filled in with a metal of a contrasting color. Originally damask meant simply a pattern of curved lines but now it is a broader term that refers to any of the lovely patterns woven into linen.

The Echeverria looks especially attractive with a patterned fabric.

★★ Instructions

1. *Fold the napkin in thirds.*

2. *Place it so the folded edge is at the top.*

3. *Hold your finger in the center of the top edge as you fold down the left and right sides.*

4. *On the right side, fold up the end that extends below the triangle in two folds so it is even with the bottom edge of the triangle.*

5. *Fold up the left side the same way.*

6. *Fold the shape in thirds by bringing the right side over the left side.*

7. *Tuck the left corner in the right fold. Turn the napkin over and stand it up.*

Echo

A home economist writing in 1921 suggested white linen place mats and matching napkins 14 to 17 inches square as the proper table setting for a luncheon. She went on to say that the cloth of which they were made should be unadorned except for the pattern of the linen. Fortunately today we have the choice of white or colors, patterned or plain, for our table settings. The Echo is a fold that can be made with a great variety of fabrics.

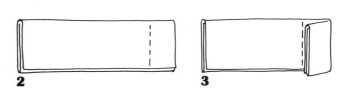

1 **2** **3**

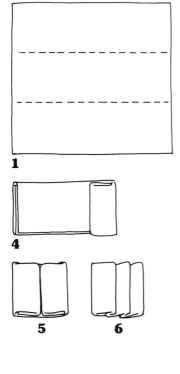

4

5 **6**

★★★ Instructions

1. *Fold the napkin in thirds.*
2. *Place it so the folded edge is at the top.*
3. *Fold the right edge over about two inches.*
4. *Bring the new right edge to the center.*
5. *Repeat steps 3 and 4 with the left side.*
6. *Fold the right side under the left side. Now there will be three folded edges on the right side. Hold the bottommost folded edge with your right hand. With your left hand separate the three folded edges.*

Elegante

When the Princess Royal of the Netherlands died in 1660, she bequeathed all her household linens to her son, the Prince of Orange. One set alone consisted of three tablecloths and 76 napkins. Whether or not you come from royal lineage, having your napkins monogrammed is certainly a regal touch. To embroider your own initial, see page 118.

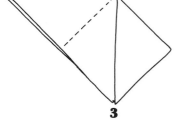

1

2

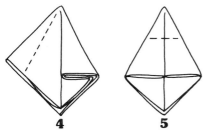

3

★★ Instructions

1. *Fold the napkin in half diagonally to form a triangle.*

2. *Arrange the napkin so the fold is on top. If your napkins have an embroidered design or a monogram in one corner, place this corner face down at the bottom of the triangle so the design will be on the outside when the fold is completed.*

3. *Fold the side edges in so they meet in the center.*

4. *Bring the right point to the center.*

5. *Bring the left point to the center.*

6. *Fold down the top point about four inches and turn the napkin over.*

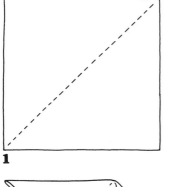

4　　　**5**　　　**6**

Emerald

Irish linen is noted for its luster, sheen, lovely natural color, and endurance, and the climate in Ireland makes it an ideal place to grow flax, from which linen is made. No other vegetable fiber has the tensile strength of flax, which gives linen its great resistance to wear and tear. It seems only natural that linen has come to be the most commonly used fabric for tablecloths and napkins.

Linen napkins folded in the Emerald shape make a handsome addition to any table.

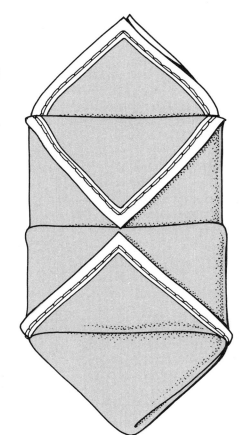

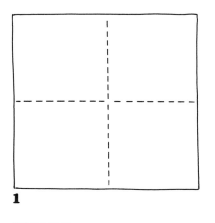

1

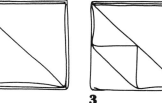

2   **3**

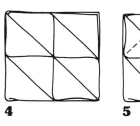

4   **5**

★★ Instructions

1. Fold the napkin in quarters.
2. Place it so the free corners are at the upper right. Fold the top right corner of the first layer to the lower left corner.
3. Fold up the same corner point so it is even with the center diagonal fold.
4. Fold down the top right corner of the next layer to meet the center fold.
5. Fold under the bottom right and top left corners.

Erin

Few American Colonists had the luxury of a separate dining room since their living space was at a premium, so they ate their meals on a board laid on trestles. The tablecloth was called a board cloth. Only the more well-to-do Colonists had a dormant table—one that remained in place between meals. But no Colonists, well-to-do or struggling, had napkins. Had they enjoyed that amenity, the simplicity of the Erin would no doubt have made it a popular fold.

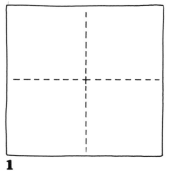

1   **2**   **3**

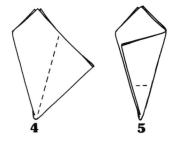

4   **5**

★★ Instructions

1. *Fold the napkin in quarters.*
2. *Place it so the free points are on the top.*
3. *Fold over the right point, as shown.*
4. *Turn the napkin over and fold over the new right point.*
5. *Fold up the bottom point and place the napkin in a mug or glass.*

Flamingo

Although the Flamingo requires quite a few steps, it is easy to master. This shape looks best when folded with a napkin that has a contrasting decorative border on all four sides.

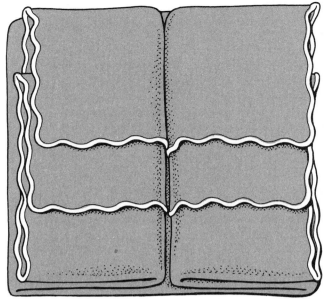

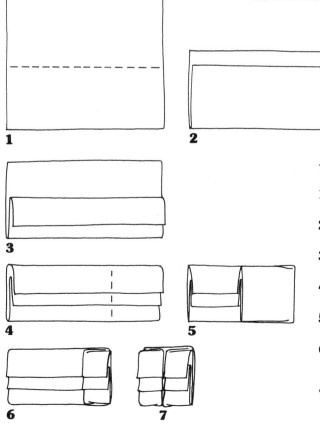

★★ Instructions

1. Lay the napkin on the table with the wrong side (if there is one) up.
2. Fold the bottom edge to within one inch of the top edge.
3. Now fold the same edge back to within one inch of the bottom.
4. Fold the top of the napkin down to within one inch of the free edge.
5. Fold two-thirds of the right half of the napkin toward the left side.
6. Now fold what was the right edge back so it is even with the fold on the right edge.
7. Repeat steps 5 and 6 with the left side.

Fleur-de-lis

Like the graceful fleur-de-lis, fancifully folded napkins have long been associated with France. Louis XIV, in particular, was enamored of their look and on festive occasions his tables were always set with napkins folded into three-dimensional shapes. The task of folding fell to the pastry cook who so impressed Louis XIV that he honored him with the title of Officer of the Household and gave him a special uniform to wear. The cook created such elaborate sculptural shapes that it was considered a breach of etiquette for a guest to unfold one of his creations.

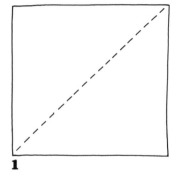

1

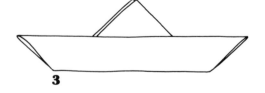

2

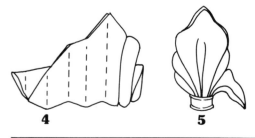

3

4   5

★★★ Instructions

1. *Fold the napkin in half diagonally to form a triangle.*
2. *Place the napkin so the folded edge is at the bottom.*
3. *Fold up the bottom edge one-third the total height of the triangle.*
4. *Turn the napkin over and fold it into one-inch-wide accordian pleats.*
5. *Slip the bottom edge into a napkin ring and pull out the points on either side.*

Flower Basket

As implied by its name, the Flower Basket lends itself beautifully to holding a blossom. It also looks especially pretty when folded with a fringed napkin.

By the middle of the sixteenth century, the linen woven for tablecloths and napkins was often ornamented. Fringed edges, lace insets, and lavish embroidery were especially popular, and in some parts of Europe white linen had given way to bright colors.

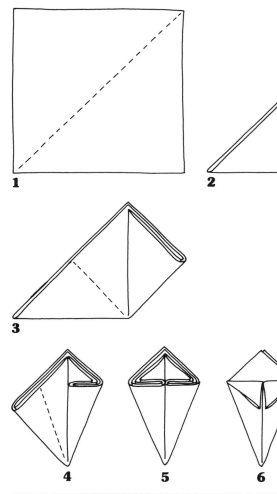

★★★ Instructions

1. *Fold the napkin in half diagonally to form a triangle.*

2. *Place it so the fold is along the bottom edge.*

3. *Bring the right and left points up to the center point.*

4. *Then fold the bottom right edge to the center.*

5. *Fold the bottom left edge to the center.*

6. *At the top of the napkin, fold down the corner points of the top layer.*

Flower Pot

The unusual looking Flower Pot is easy to fold. It was included in a Swedish book on table settings published in the early part of the twentieth century. This shape works best with a cloth napkin, and it is appropriate for any meal.

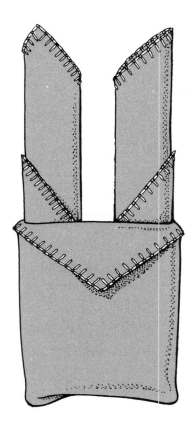

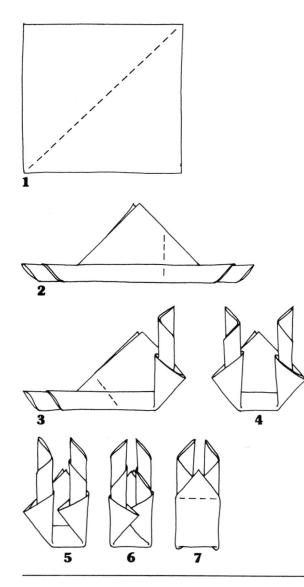

★★★ Instructions

1. *Fold the napkin in half diagonally to form a triangle.*
2. *Place the napkin so the fold is along the bottom edge. Starting at the bottom edge, roll up the napkin slightly more than halfway.*
3. *Hold your fingers about four inches apart at the center of the bottom edge and fold up the right point perpendicular to the bottom edge.*
4. *Repeat with the left point.*
5. *Fold in the right side leaving the center point of the napkin just visible.*
6. *Fold in the left side.*
7. *Turn the napkin over and fold down the center point.*

Fortunella

In times past, the proper napkin fold for informal meals such as breakfast, lunch, buffet supper or afternoon tea was simple but strict. The napkin was first folded in quarters and then in half to form a triangle, and the triangle was placed with the fold parallel to the fork and the point facing out. The formal dinner napkin, which measured 22 inches square, was folded in thirds lengthwise and then in thirds crosswise to form a smaller square. Fortunately, the strict rules of times past have given way to a greater informality. The Fortunella, a simple fold, is appropriate for any meal.

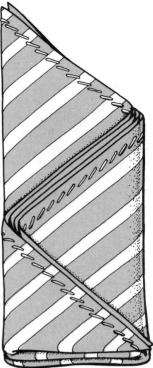

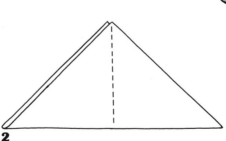

1 **2**

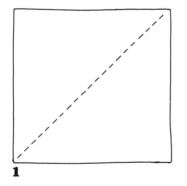

fold

3 **4**

★ Instructions

1. Fold the napkin in half diagonally to from a triangle.

2. Place the triangle so the fold is along the bottom edge.

3. Fold the triangle in half by bringing the left point over to the right point.

4. Fold the right point back toward the left, leaving one-third of the napkin under the fold. Turn the same point back to the right edge.

Hyacinth

Its tall shape makes the Hyacinth a good fold to use if the napkins are to play an important role in your table decoration. The fold, attractive in either a floral print or a solid color napkin, needs a sturdy napkin ring for a base.

In medieval times, not only were there no napkin rings, but table utensils were limited to spoons, provided by the guests themselves. Each guest brought his own spoon whether he was invited for one meal or a one-month visit. Most spoons were made of carved wood or tin, but those of the wealthy were wrought in ornamented silver. The importance of the spoon made it a perfect baby gift—hence the saying, "Born with a silver spoon in his mouth."

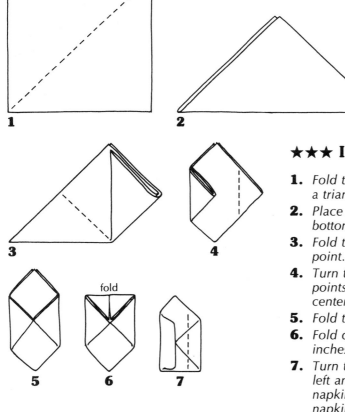

★★★ Instructions

1. Fold the napkin in half diagonally to form a triangle.
2. Place the napkin so the fold is along the bottom edge.
3. Fold the right and left points up to the top point.
4. Turn the napkin over, keeping the free points at the top. Fold the left point to the center.
5. Fold the right point to meet the left point.
6. Fold down the top point about four inches.
7. Turn the napkin upside down. Fold the left and right sides to the center. Turn the napkin over and set the bottom edge in a napkin ring.

Iris

Although it is customary to place the napkin to the left of the fork, many etiquette books from the late nineteenth and early twentieth centuries state that the proper place is to the *right* of the plate. At your next dinner party, why not fold napkins in the Iris shape and place them to the right of the plates.

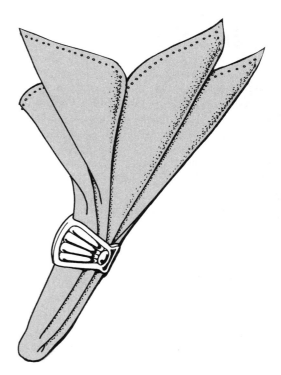

1

2

★★★ Instructions

1. *Fold the napkin in half diagonally to form a triangle.*

2. *Place the napkin so the fold is along the bottom edge.*

3. *Bring the right and then the left point up to the center point.*

4. *Fold the lower right edge to the center.*

5. *Repeat with the lower left edge.*

6. *Fold the napkin in half by bringing the right side back under the left side. Slip the bottom three inches of the napkin through a napkin ring and separate the top points slightly.*

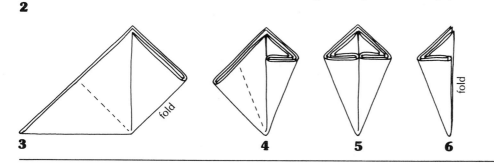

3 **4** **5** **6**

Irish Ripples

In the middle of the nineteenth century, the word doily was used to describe a small colored napkin used only after eating fruit or candy. Today colored napkins are used throughout the meal. Irish Ripples is especially attractive with a napkin that contrasts with the color of the tablecloth.

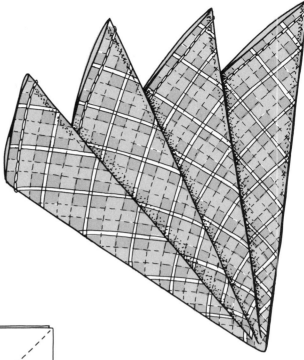

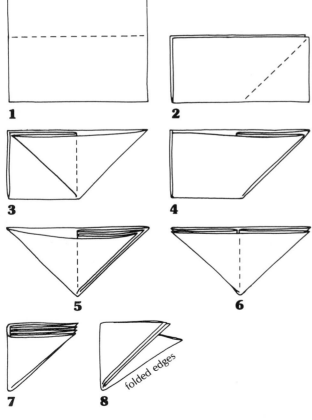

★★★ Instructions

1. *Fold the napkin in half to form a rectangle.*
2. *Place it so the fold is along the bottom edge.*
3. *Bring the top layer of the upper right corner over to the top left corner.*
4. *Now bring what was the top layer of the upper right corner back to its original position on the right.*
5. *Now bring the top layer of the upper left corner over to the upper right corner.*
6. *Bring the upper left corner back to its original position.*
7. *Fold the napkin in half.*
8. *Separate each of the corner points slightly.*

Lily

The advent of the fork, which made eating neater and more manageable, was probably a great influence on the upgrading of table linens as well. Italians first made use of that ingenious piece of cutlery in the sixteenth century, but before long other Europeans were following suit. In England, when forks were included as part of a place setting, the innovation caused such a furor that the custom was denounced from the pulpit. But forks were here to stay.

What better way to show off beautiful linen napkins than by folding them in the Lily.

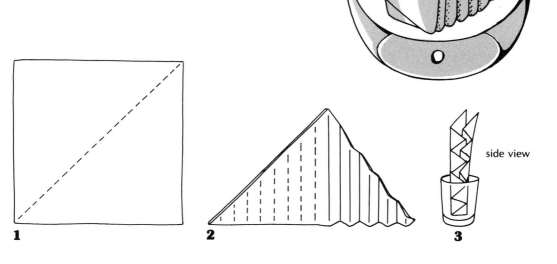

1   **2**   **3**   side view

★★ Instructions

1. *Fold the napkin in half diagonally to form a triangle.*

2. *Place the napkin so the folded edge is along the bottom and fold the napkin into one-inch accordian pleats.*

3. *Place the base of the napkin in a glass and separate the layers of the napkin to make two petals.*

Mexican Fan

To flaunt your beautiful damask napkins at your next dinner party, fold them into Mexican Fans. Linen damask is a firm, lustrous fabric with a woven-in design made on a jacquard loom. Double damask has about twice as many filling, or crosswise, threads as single damask, but if it has a low thread count, it will not wear as well as a single damask of good quality with a high count.

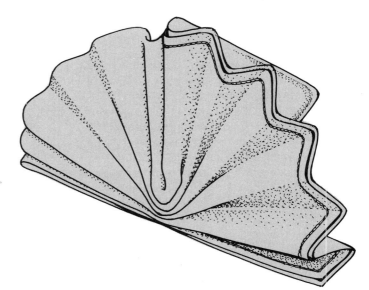

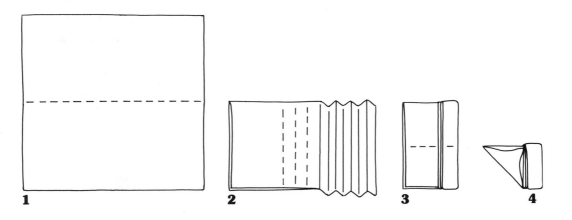

1　　**2**　　**3**　　**4**

★★★ Instructions

1. *Fold the napkin in half to make a rectangle.*
2. *Fold the napkin into one-inch accordian pleats leaving, the last four inches unfolded.*
3. *Fold in half, with the pleats on the outside.*
4. *Fold up the bottom left corner and tuck it into the pleats. Stand the napkin up so the pleats form a fan.*

Monogram

As the name implies, the Monogram is a perfect fold for displaying the family initial. To embroider your initial, see page 118.

According to one source, the proper number of table linens for a hostess to have includes: a white damask tablecloth and matching dinner napkins at least 19 inches square, three or four printed tablecloths for breakfast and lunch, three lace or embroidered tablecloths with two dozen 14-inch-square napkins for afternoon tea, three dozen cocktail napkins, and two dozen finger bowl doilies.

1

2

3

4

5   **6**

★★★ Instructions

1. Fold the napkin in half diagonally to form a triangle, with the monogram face down in the center of the bottom point.

2. Place the folded edge at the top.

3. Hold your finger in the center of the top edge and fold over the right point, as shown.

4. With your finger still in place, bring the same point back to the right side making a fold that is straight down the center of the napkin.

5. Then bring the right point down to the bottom point.

6. Repeat steps 3 through 5 with the left side. Turn the napkin over.

New Square

Catherine Beecher would have liked the New Square for its practicality. In 1841 she wrote *A Treatise on Domestic Economy* that became a best seller. In it she stated that a stranger must always have a clean napkin but that members of a family should reuse their napkins until they were completely soiled. She suggested that a napkin could be folded so that, even if partially soiled, a clean side could be turned out. This could be done two more times before laundering was necessary.

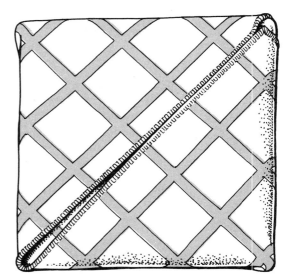

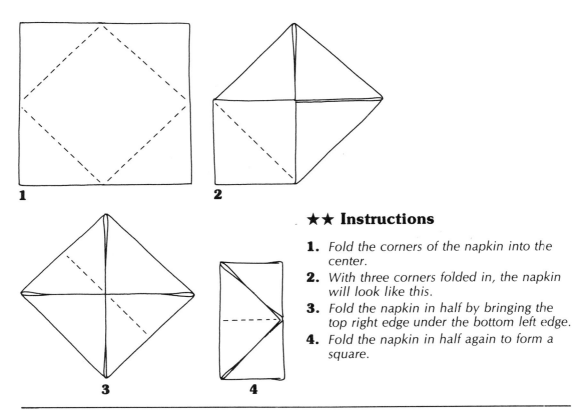

1 **2**

3 **4**

★★ Instructions

1. *Fold the corners of the napkin into the center.*
2. *With three corners folded in, the napkin will look like this.*
3. *Fold the napkin in half by bringing the top right edge under the bottom left edge.*
4. *Fold the napkin in half again to form a square.*

Obelisk

History tells us that the first napkin appeared on the table of Charles VII in his palace in Reims, France. From the beginning of the fifteenth century, napkins were a luxury used exclusively by royalty. They were made of lovely linen damask and often elaborately embroidered with monograms, coats-of-arms, and other royal insignia.

Although the simple Obelisk was probably not used in royal courts, it can be folded with a linen damask, printed cotton, or even a paper napkin.

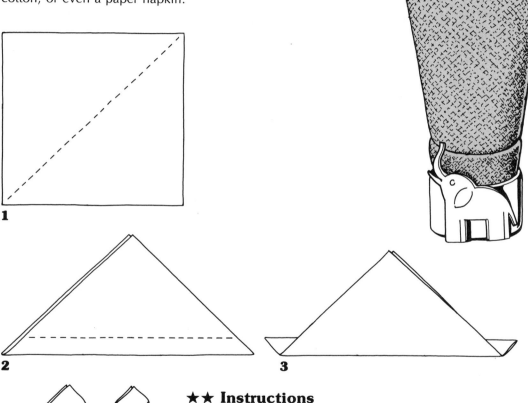

1

2

3

4

5

★★ Instructions

1. Fold the napkin in half diagonally to form a triangle.

2. Place the triangle with the fold at the base. Fold up two inches along the bottom edge.

3. Turn the napkin over.

4. Starting at the right end, roll the right half into the center. Starting at the left edge, begin to roll up the left side.

5. Roll up the left side until it meets the rolled right side. Turn the napkin over and slip the base into a napkin ring.

Orchid

The Orchid is a beautiful fold to use with linen napkins.

Linen, according to an etiquette book of 1921, should be introduced to children as early as possible. The book suggested that each child have a linen damask napkin, a silver napkin ring with his monogram, and matching clips for holding the napkin in place around his neck. Gone are those days, but people of any age appreciate fine linen.

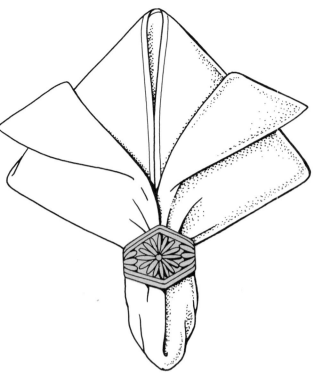

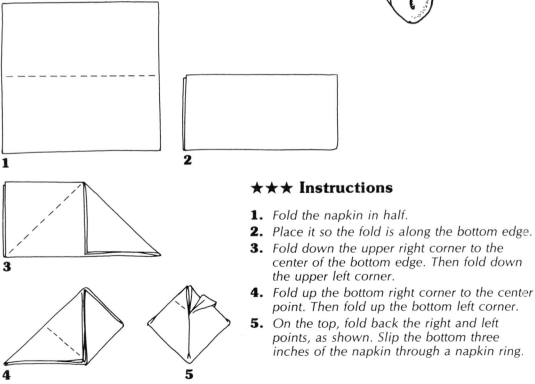

★★★ Instructions

1. *Fold the napkin in half.*
2. *Place it so the fold is along the bottom edge.*
3. *Fold down the upper right corner to the center of the bottom edge. Then fold down the upper left corner.*
4. *Fold up the bottom right corner to the center point. Then fold up the bottom left corner.*
5. *On the top, fold back the right and left points, as shown. Slip the bottom three inches of the napkin through a napkin ring.*

Palm Frond

The Palm Frond is a very easy shape to fold and looks especially elegant when made with a large—at least 20-inches-square—linen napkin and placed in a tall wine glass.

In the early sixteenth century when the Belgian towns of Flanders and Ypres were the centers of the linen weaving trade, the industry was under a strict guild system. Each shipment of linen bore a seal guaranteeing its quality and measurement. In those days a napkin measured one ell and a half—an ell is the length from one's elbow to the tip of the middle finger. Such a large napkin would make a luxurious Palm Frond.

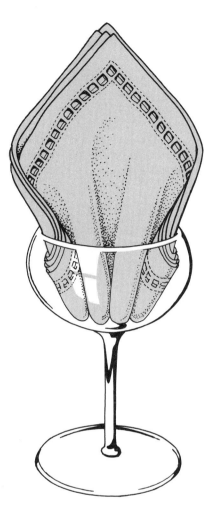

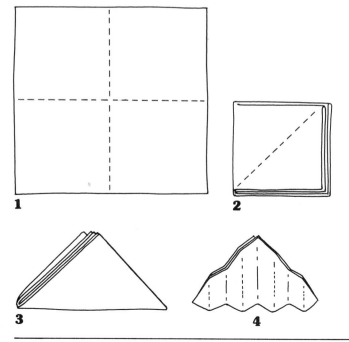

★ Instructions

1. *Fold the napkin in quarters.*
2. *Place the napkin so the free corners are at the bottom right.*
3. *Fold it in half diagonally to form a triangle. Place the napkin so this fold is along the bottom edge.*
4. *Accordian-pleat the triangle into soft one-inch pleats; do not press the pleats. Place the bottom edge of the triangle in a glass and let the folds above the rim open slightly.*

Party Hat

A table set with napkins folded into Party Hats makes a festive setting for any informal gathering. The shape stands up best when made with large—at least 20-inch-square—napkins in a crisp, thick fabric.

Napkins were often eliminated from the table when forks were first used because diners' hands stayed so clean that napkins seemed superfluous.

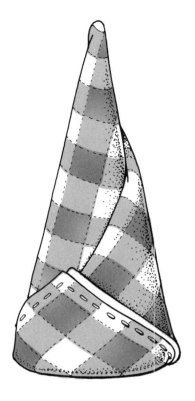

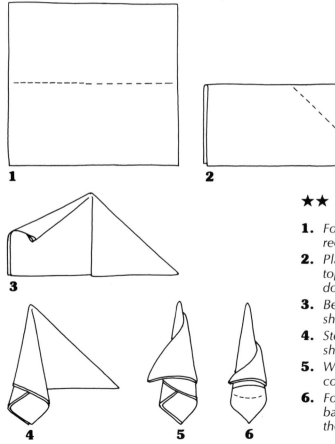

★★ Instructions

1. *Fold the napkin in half to form a rectangle.*

2. *Place the napkin so the fold is along the top edge. Bring the top right corner down to the center of the bottom edge.*

3. *Begin to roll the napkin into a cone shape starting at the top left corner.*

4. *Stop rolling when the cone is vertical, as shown.*

5. *Wrap the bottom right corner around the cone.*

6. *Fold up the point that extends below the base of the cone, making sure it covers the bottom right point. Stand up the hat.*

Party Wheel

The festive look of the Party Wheel can turn a family dinner into a celebration. To make the pleats fan out into a circle, you must use a very narrow napkin ring, a napkin clip, or a ribbon tied around the center of the napkin as shown in the drawing at right.

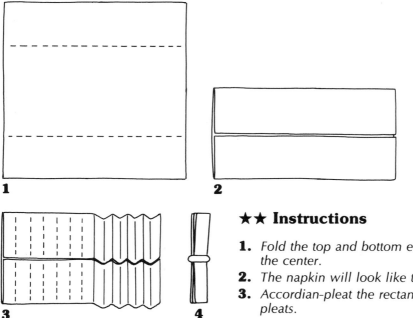

1

2

3

4

★★ Instructions

1. *Fold the top and bottom edges of the napkin to the center.*
2. *The napkin will look like this.*
3. *Accordian-pleat the rectangle into one-inch pleats.*
4. *Slip a napkin ring or napkin clip around the center of the napkin or tie a ribbon around it. Fan out the pleats to make a wheel shape.*

Peacock

As table linens evolved so did rules governing their use. One English publication of the seventeenth century boasted twenty-five ways of folding a napkin, complete with diagrams. The Peacock was not among them, but it would do any table proud. It can be folded with either a cloth or a large paper napkin.

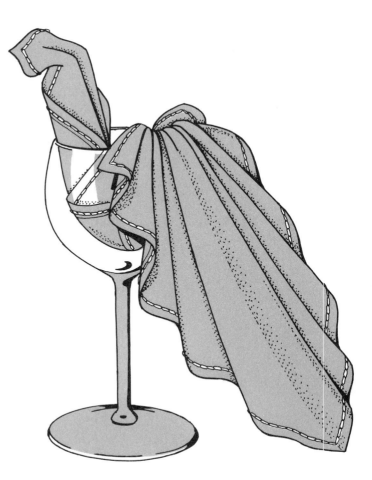

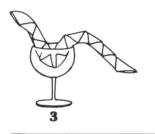

1

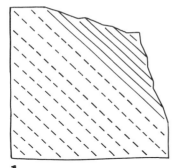

2

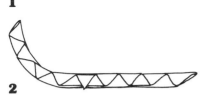

3

★★★ Instructions

1. *Fold the napkin in one-inch accordian pleats, folding diagonally from the bottom left to the upper right corner.*

2. *Bend the resulting pleated shape at a point about six inches in from one end.*

3. *Place the bend of the napkin in a glass so that both the short (head) and long (tail) ends protrude above the rim. Fan out the pleats slightly to form the tail and adjust the head.*

Peony

The Peony can be folded with a cloth or paper napkin, but it looks elegant on a table set with lovely silverware.

In the seventeenth century, silver flatware, a sign of riches, was often presented to a child at birth. Samuel Pepys noted in his *Diary* that he purchased six spoons and a plate for a child to be named after him. When the baby was christened John, Pepys thought better of his extravagance and carried home the spoons and plate.

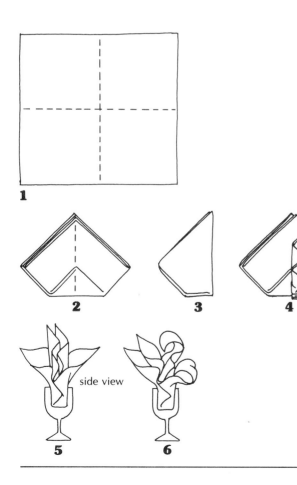

side view

★★★ Instructions

1. *Fold the napkin in quarters.*
2. *Place the napkin so the free corners are at the top, then fold up the bottom corner about three inches.*
3. *Fold the napkin in half vertically.*
4. *Accordian-pleat each half separately to the center.*
5. *Place the bottom of the napkin in a glass and separate the four layers.*
6. *Tuck in the corner points of each layer to form the petals.*

Philodendron

In the May 1890 issue of *Cornhill*, a British magazine, the household editor said, "The abominable fashion of discarding the white tablecloth in favor of red or other colors is distinctly Yankee. . . . The hostess was probably influenced in choice of color by what looks good on her rather than what suits the table." The British editor might have felt differently if the tablecloth had been accompanied by coordinated printed napkins folded in the Philodendron shape.

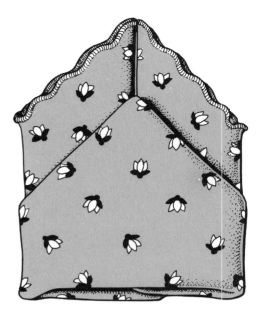

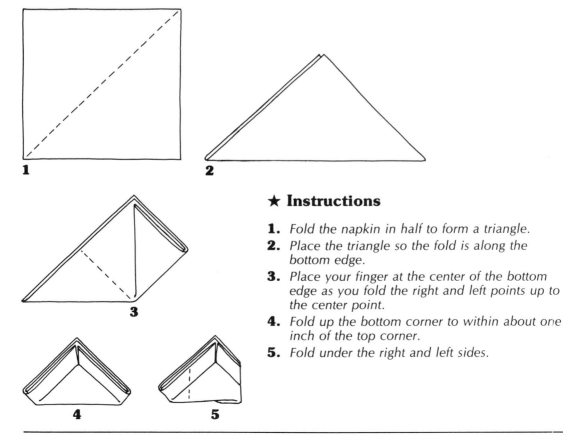

1

2

3

4

5

★ Instructions

1. *Fold the napkin in half to form a triangle.*

2. *Place the triangle so the fold is along the bottom edge.*

3. *Place your finger at the center of the bottom edge as you fold the right and left points up to the center point.*

4. *Fold up the bottom corner to within about one inch of the top corner.*

5. *Fold under the right and left sides.*

Phoenix

The Phoenix must be folded with a cloth napkin of linen, cotton, or a blend. The advice of one writer on household management at the turn of the century remains valid today. A fine-thread linen damask, she said, may not be the most durable. The best fabric is firm, not too fine or stiff with starch; it should have an elastic, "leathery" appearance. Patterns with long threads on top are less durable than patterns with shorter expanses of thread; damask with a less showy design is more durable.

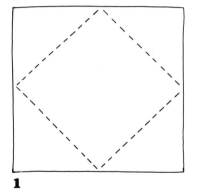

1

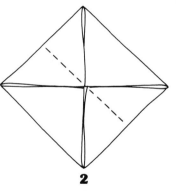

2

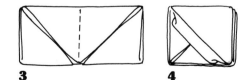

3   **4**

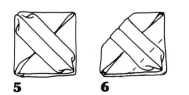

5   **6**

★★★ Instructions

1. *Fold the corners of the napkin to the center.*

2. *The napkin will look like this.*

3. *Fold the napkin in half by bringing the bottom edge under top edge.*

4. *Fold the napkin in half again. Starting at the top right corner, roll under the first layer of the napkin.*

5. *Roll the second layer in the opposite direction.*

6. *Fold under the top left and bottom right corners.*

Pineapple

An 1895 catalog from Harrod's, London's famous department store, offered both 17- and 24-inch-square luncheon napkins with a variety of edgings such as hemstitching and openwork embroidery. Any decoratively edged napkin is appropriate for folding the Pineapple, which makes a vivid impression when standing at each place setting.

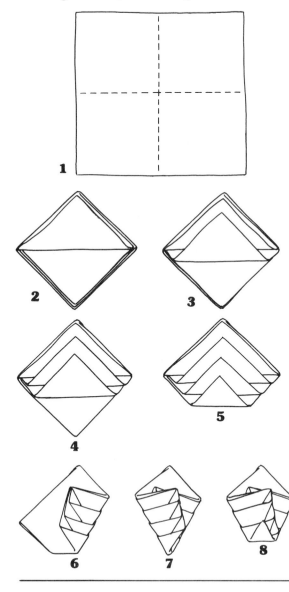

★★★ Instructions

1. Fold the napkin in quarters.

2. Place it so the free corners are at the bottom. Fold up the bottom corner of the first layer to meet the top corner.

3. Fold the bottom corner of the next layer to within one inch of the top corner.

4. Fold the bottom corner of the third layer to within one inch of the second layer.

5. Fold the bottom corner of the last layer up to within one inch of the third layer.

6. Turn the napkin over. Fold the right side diagonally over the center.

7. Fold over the left side.

8. Fold up the bottom point. Turn the napkin over and anchor it in a napkin ring.

Poinsettia

A complex fold, the Poinsettia may require a little practice. Use a 20-inch-square napkin, and, at Christmas, try the fold with bright red napkins for a festive look.

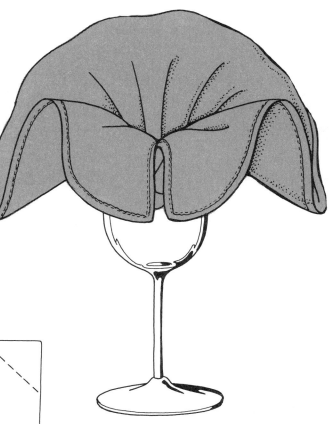

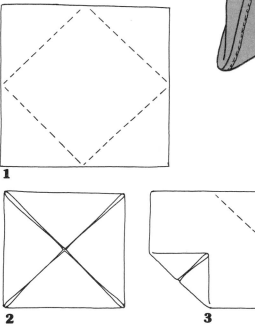

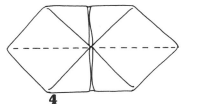

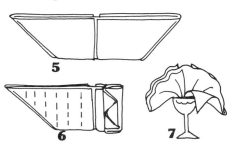

★★★★ Instructions

1. Fold the corners of the napkin to the center.
2. The napkin will look like this.
3. Carefully turn the napkin over. Bring the upper right and lower left corners to the center.
4. Place the napkin so that one long edge is at the bottom.
5. Fold the napkin in half by bringing the top edge down to the bottom edge.
6. Accordian-pleat this shape into one-inch pleats.
7. Place the bottom edge of the napkin in a glass. To curve the top, pull out and down on the left and right sides. To form the front petals, pull down on the free corners of the napkin at the center.

Pyramid

The Pyramid, a popular fold in European restaurants in the early part of this century, looks crisp and fresh when made with a white napkin. A flower or party favor can be tucked inside the shape.

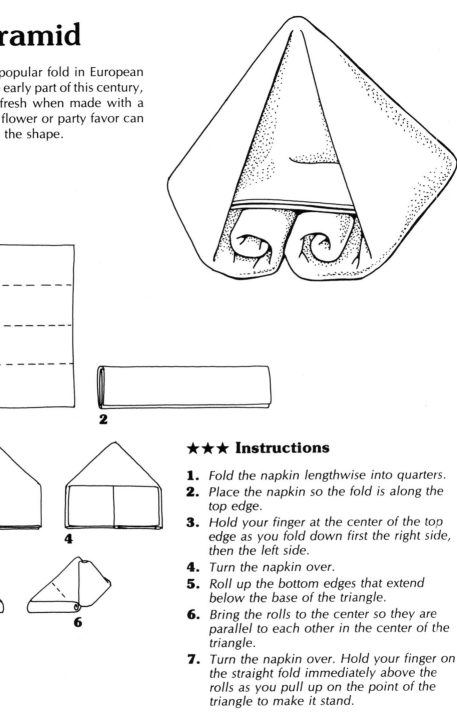

1

2

3

4

5

6

7

★★★ Instructions

1. *Fold the napkin lengthwise into quarters.*
2. *Place the napkin so the fold is along the top edge.*
3. *Hold your finger at the center of the top edge as you fold down first the right side, then the left side.*
4. *Turn the napkin over.*
5. *Roll up the bottom edges that extend below the base of the triangle.*
6. *Bring the rolls to the center so they are parallel to each other in the center of the triangle.*
7. *Turn the napkin over. Hold your finger on the straight fold immediately above the rolls as you pull up on the point of the triangle to make it stand.*

Queen Anne

According to a household manual published at the beginning of the twentieth century, the leading suppliers of table linen were Ireland, Scotland, Germany, Belgium, Austria, and France. Irish linen was considered best because it was bleached naturally in the sun; artificial bleaching methods reduce the weight and strength of the fabric. The Queen Anne will beautifully show off linen napkins.

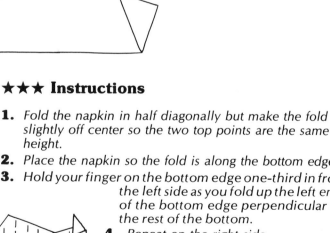

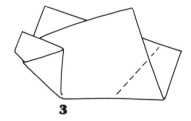

1

2

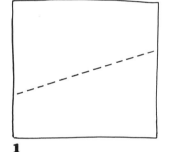

3

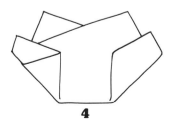

4

5

★★★ Instructions

1. *Fold the napkin in half diagonally but make the fold slightly off center so the two top points are the same height.*

2. *Place the napkin so the fold is along the bottom edge.*

3. *Hold your finger on the bottom edge one-third in from the left side as you fold up the left end of the bottom edge perpendicular to the rest of the bottom.*

4. *Repeat on the right side.*

5. *Accordian-pleat this shape into one-inch pleats. Place the bottom of the napkin in a glass and let the pleats above the rim fan out slightly.*

Reflections

Reflections is an easy shape to fold and so versatile that it looks good when folded with a solid, printed, or striped napkin. You can set a place card across the bottom or tuck it under the lower point.

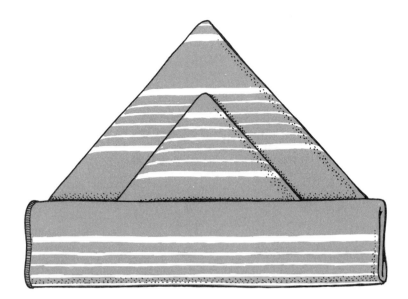

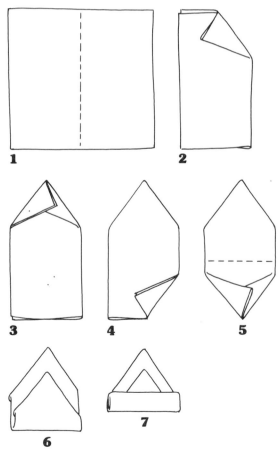

★★★ Instructions

1. *Fold the napkin in half to form a rectangle.*
2. *Hold your finger at the center of the top edge as you fold the top right corner across the center of the napkin.*
3. *Fold down the top left corner so it overlaps the right corner.*
4. *Turn the napkin over and fold up the bottom right corner in the same way.*
5. *Fold up the bottom left corner so it overlaps the right corner.*
6. *Bring the bottom point up to within one inch of the top point.*
7. *Fold up about two inches of the bottom edge.*

Regimental Stripe

Although this fold requires quite a few steps, it is easy to master and makes a shape elegant enough to place on your best china. It looks good in the center of the plate or to the left of the forks.

In her *Household Management* (1905), Bertha Terrill said, "There is a happy medium between the huge chests of linen in former times which held supplies not used for years, yellowing with age, and the modern tendency to hand-to-mouth provision, satisfying only the weekly demand. There should always be a small emergency store of linen." She describes such a store as three tablecloths and four dozen napkins.

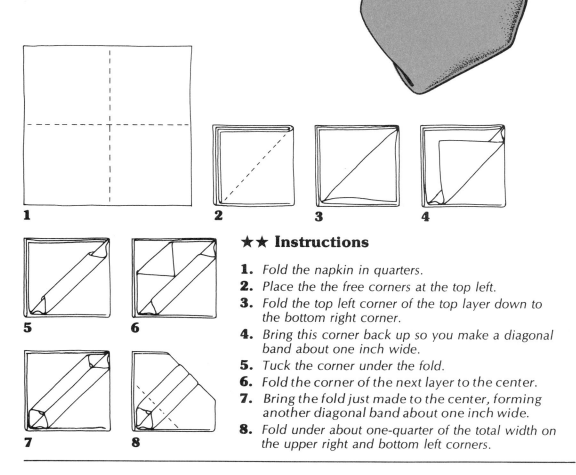

★★ Instructions

1. Fold the napkin in quarters.
2. Place the the free corners at the top left.
3. Fold the top left corner of the top layer down to the bottom right corner.
4. Bring this corner back up so you make a diagonal band about one inch wide.
5. Tuck the corner under the fold.
6. Fold the corner of the next layer to the center.
7. Bring the fold just made to the center, forming another diagonal band about one inch wide.
8. Fold under about one-quarter of the total width on the upper right and bottom left corners.

Rio

An American etiquette book published in 1923 states that the napkin should be folded into a square and placed one inch from the edge of the table, square to the table edge and to the forks, with the open corners at the lower right. Today's less stringent rules allow for great variety, including lovely folds like the Rio.

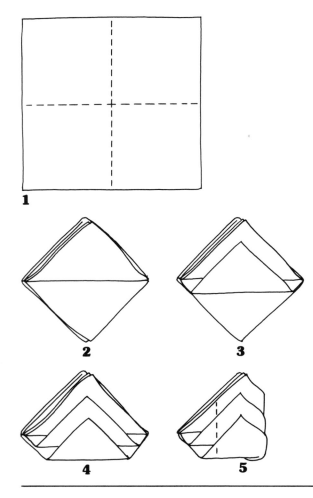

★★ Instructions

1. *Fold the napkin in quarters.*
2. *Place the napkin on a diagonal so the free corners are at the bottom. Fold the top two layers of the bottom corner to the top corner.*
3. *Fold the bottom corner of the third layer to within one inch of the top corner.*
4. *Fold the bottom corner of the fourth layer to within one inch of the third layer.*
5. *Fold under the right and left sides.*

Rose

The Rose was a favorite fold of Escoffier's, the noted French chef of the last century who helped to make table decoration an art. Use a 20-inch-square napkin to fold the Rose.

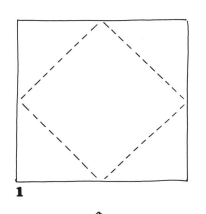

1

2

3

4

5

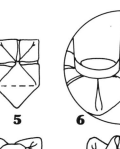

6

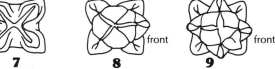

7

8 front

9 front

★★★★ Instructions

1. *Fold the corners of the napkin to the center.*
2. *The napkin will look like this.*
3. *Fold the new corners to the center.*
4. *Again, fold the corners to the center.*
5. *Carefully holding the center, turn the napkin over. Then fold the corners to the center.*
6. *Place a glass on the center of the napkin to anchor it as you pull out the corners from the underside. Give a slight tug on each corner to make it stand up.*
7. *When all four corners have been pulled out, remove the glass. Hold on to the center points as you turn the napkin over.*
8. *Hold these points together on the underside while you pull out a point on each side at the front.*
9. *Then fluff out the innermost points to form the center petals.*

Rugby

Napkins folded in the Rugby shape are a perfect addition to the table set for an informal meal, a lunch, or an outdoor supper.

In the Middle Ages, tablecloths reached nearly to the floor, serving as both tablecovers and napkins. Guests simply used the overhanging cloth to wipe hands and mouth. Since forks had not yet been introduced, a bowl of water was passed around between courses so diners could wash their hands. Our present-day fingerbowls are the only trace that remains of this early custom.

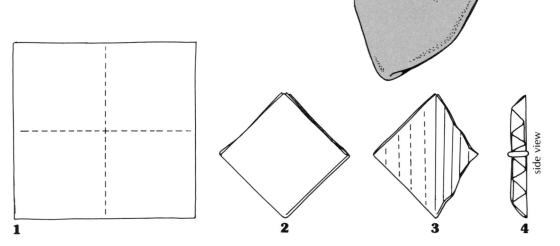

side view

1 **2** **3** **4**

★★ Instructions

1. Fold the napkin in quarters.

2. Place it so the free corners are at the top and the folded corner is at the bottom.

3. Accordian-pleat this diamond shape into one-inch pleats.

4. Secure the pleats by slipping the napkin through a napkin ring or tie a ribbon around the middle.

Sapphire

Although the Sapphire must be folded with a 20-inch-square cloth napkin, the end result is a dainty shape that will enhance any table set for breakfast, lunch, or dinner. The Sapphire lends itself well to both printed and solid fabrics.

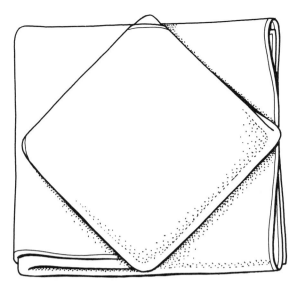

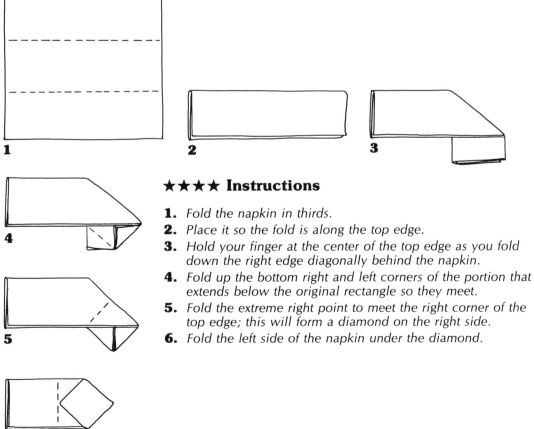

★★★★ Instructions

1. *Fold the napkin in thirds.*
2. *Place it so the fold is along the top edge.*
3. *Hold your finger at the center of the top edge as you fold down the right edge diagonally behind the napkin.*
4. *Fold up the bottom right and left corners of the portion that extends below the original rectangle so they meet.*
5. *Fold the extreme right point to meet the right corner of the top edge; this will form a diamond on the right side.*
6. *Fold the left side of the napkin under the diamond.*

Swedish Bayonets

Swedish Bayonets, a very unusual shape and a challenge to fold, comes from *Tablecloths and Napkins,* a Swedish book published in the early part of the twentieth century. The book recommends using a large, starched napkin. Swedish Bayonets is one of the few folds in this book that would benefit from a light starch. Use a 20-inch or larger square cloth napkin.

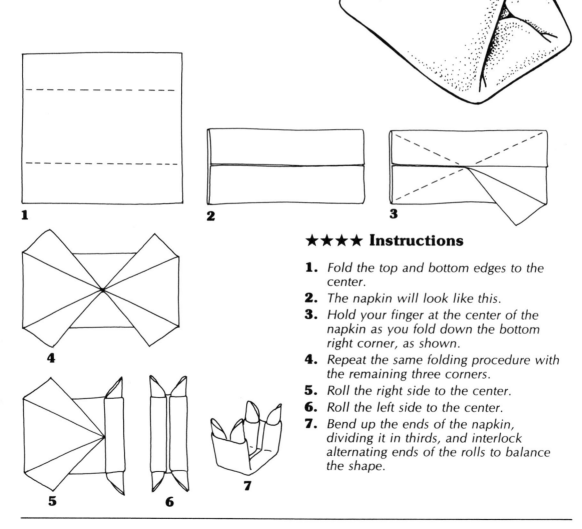

1

2

3

4

5   **6**

7

★★★★ Instructions

1. Fold the top and bottom edges to the center.

2. The napkin will look like this.

3. Hold your finger at the center of the napkin as you fold down the bottom right corner, as shown.

4. Repeat the same folding procedure with the remaining three corners.

5. Roll the right side to the center.

6. Roll the left side to the center.

7. Bend up the ends of the napkin, dividing it in thirds, and interlock alternating ends of the rolls to balance the shape.

Tavern

In the early days, most well-to-do American Colonists boasted tablecloths of white linen damask but napkins were non-existent. At that time, it was customary for guests and family to wipe hands and mouth on the edge of the tablecloth, a rather unattractive convention by today's standards.

Napkins folded in the Tavern shape are a lovely addition to any table and they certainly reflect good manners.

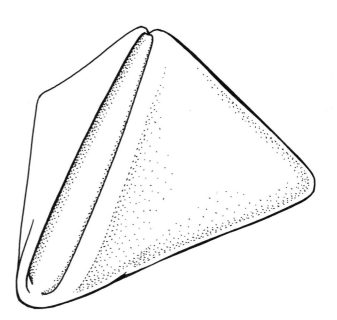

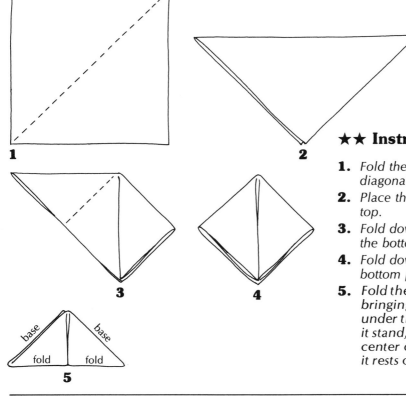

★★ Instructions

1. Fold the napkin in half diagonally to form a triangle.
2. Place the folded edge at the top.
3. Fold down the right point to the bottom point.
4. Fold down the left point to the bottom point.
5. Fold the napkin in half by bringing the bottom point under the top point. To make it stand, lift the napkin at the center of the bottom edge so it rests on the two side edges.

Temple Bells

In late seventeenth century England, it was common practice to fold linen napkins in decorative shapes resembling animals or flowers. Samuel Pepys noted in his *Diary* that he was so pleased with the custom that he was going to pay someone 40 shillings to teach his wife to make these elaborate shapes. The classic beauty of Temple Bells would inspire anyone to try it.

1

2

3

4

5

6

7

★★★★ Instructions

1. *Fold the napkin in half diagonally.*

2. *Place the fold at the bottom.*

3. *Hold your finger at the center of the bottom edge as you fold up the left and right points so they align with the center point.*

4. *Fold up the bottom point about four inches.*

5. *Fold down the same point so it is even with the bottom edge.*

6. *Accordian-pleat the shape into one-inch pleats.*

7. *Place the base of the napkin in the glass, keeping the bottom point outside the rim. Pull out the sides to form petals.*

Tulip

The intricate design of the Tulip is shown to best advantage if the shape is folded with a 20-inch-square, solid-color cloth napkin. To show off the fold, place it at the center of a plate. If your plates have a floral pattern, try to make the Tulip with coordinating pastel napkins.

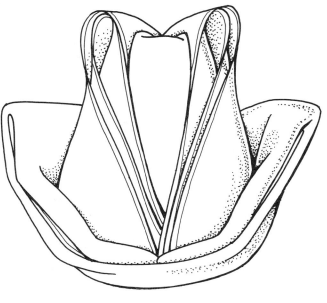

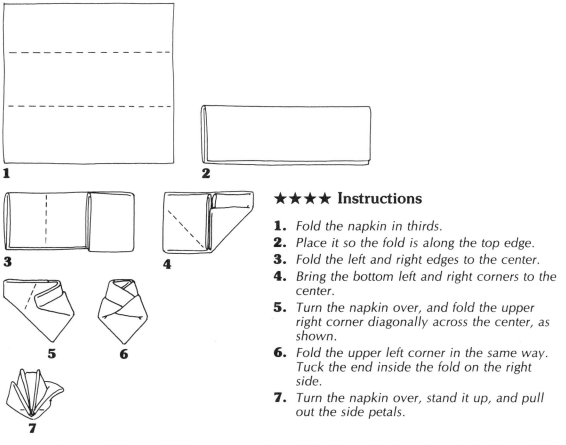

★★★★ Instructions

1. Fold the napkin in thirds.
2. Place it so the fold is along the top edge.
3. Fold the left and right edges to the center.
4. Bring the bottom left and right corners to the center.
5. Turn the napkin over, and fold the upper right corner diagonally across the center, as shown.
6. Fold the upper left corner in the same way. Tuck the end inside the fold on the right side.
7. Turn the napkin over, stand it up, and pull out the side petals.

Van Dyke

The Van Dyke is a simple shape that can be folded with cloth or paper napkins. In the early seventeenth century napkins began to play a decorative role in table setting. They were folded into birds, flowers, and animals. By the nineteenth century the art of folding napkins was so highly developed that the famous chef, Brillat-Savarin, claimed there were over 400 variations.

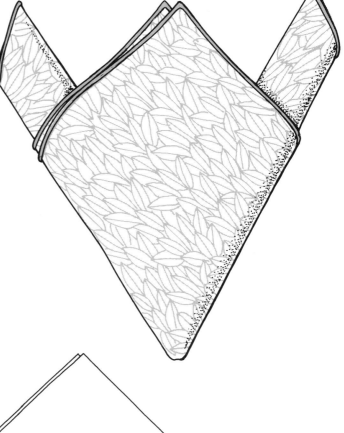

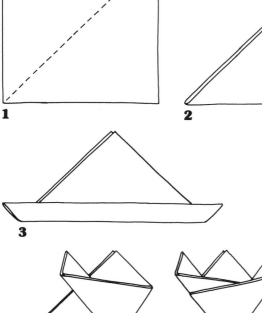

★★ Instructions

1. *Fold the napkin in half diagonally to form a triangle.*
2. *Place the triangle so the fold is along the bottom edge.*
3. *Fold up the bottom edge two inches.*
4. *Hold your finger at the center of the bottom edge as you fold up the right side.*
5. *Then fold up the left side and turn the napkin over.*

Victoria

Catherine Beecher stated in her *Treatise on Domestic Economy* (1841) that every family member should have his or her own napkin. To identify the napkins from meal to meal, she suggested using numbered napkin rings.

The Victoria is a simple but elegant way to fold a napkin to slip through a napkin ring, numbered or not.

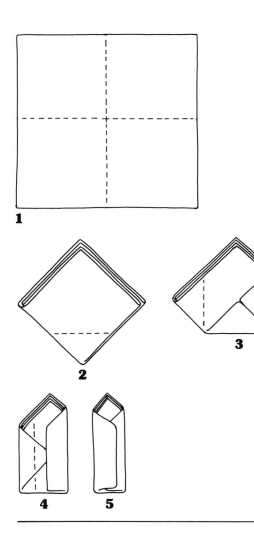

★★★ Instructions

1. *Fold the napkin in quarters.*

2. *Place it so the free corners are at the top and fold the bottom corner to the center.*

3. *Fold the left and right corners to the center.*

4. *Fold in the right side about two inches.*

5. *Fold in the left side so it slightly overlaps the right side. Turn the napkin over and slip it through a napkin ring.*

Water Lily

Isabella Mary Beeton, author of *Mrs. Beeton's Hints to Housewives,* published in 1868, advised eighteen double damask dinner napkins, each 30 inches square, for a household of four. She said it was absolutely useless to attempt anything but the simplest folds unless the napkins were slightly starched and smoothly ironed. The Water Lily is an easy but elegant fold that does not require a starched napkin—it looks best if pleated to form soft folds.

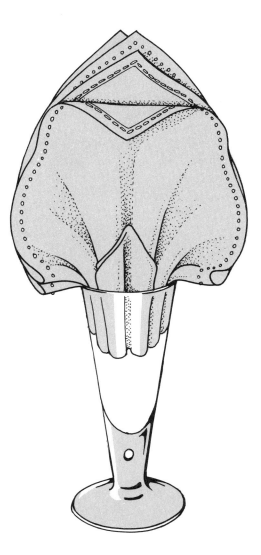

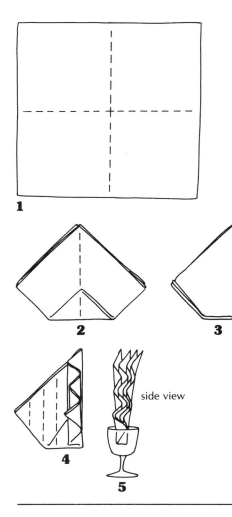

side view

★★★ Instructions

1. Fold the napkin in quarters.
2. Place it so the free corners are at the top, then fold up the bottom corner about three inches.
3. Fold the napkin in half by bringing the right edge over to the left edge.
4. Accordian-pleat each half to the center.
5. Place the bottom of the napkin in a glass and slightly separate the top corners.

Wedding Ring

The Wedding Ring is a classic shape that requires a 20-inch or larger square cloth napkin. This fold can be placed at the center of a dinner plate or to the left of the forks. Put a place card on the bottom part of the napkin below the two rings or tuck one end of the card inside a ring.

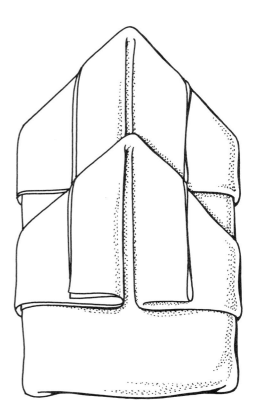

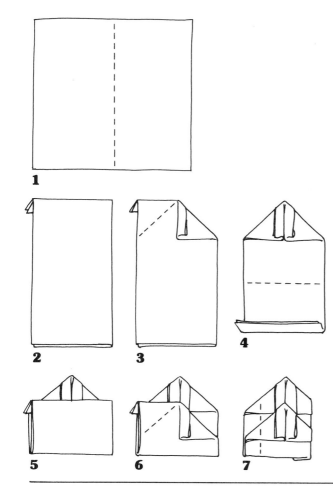

★★★★ Instructions

1. Fold the napkin in half to make a rectangle.
2. Turn under one-half inch along the top edge.
3. Hold the folded edge at the center with one hand as you fold down the top right and left corners to the center.
4. Turn up the bottom edge one-half inch.
5. Hold this folded edge as you bring it up to overlap the base of the triangle at the top by about one inch.
6. Hold the folded edge at the center as you fold down the right and left corners to the center.
7. Fold under both sides about two inches.

Wendy's Fan

White figured damask has become synonymous with linen tablecloths and napkins. This type of weaving with a woven-in pattern was developed in the fifteenth century and the earliest design was a coat-of-arms. Today damask designs are primarily floral. Wendy's Fan is a beautiful fold to use with damask napkins.

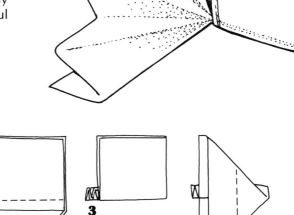

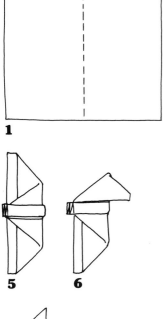

1

2

3

4

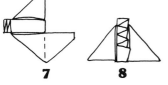

5   **6**

7   **8**

★★★★ Instructions

1. *Fold the napkin in half.*

2. *Accordian-pleat half the napkin into one-inch pleats, making the last fold one pleat beyond the center of the napkin.*

3. *Turn the napkin over.*

4. *Holding the pleats securely, bring the top layer of the top left corner down to the bottom left creating a triangle over the pleats.*

5. *Fold the right side over to the left side.*

6. *Fold down the top left edge so it lies along the upper side of the pleats, as shown. Then fold up the bottom left edge so it lies along the lower side of the pleats.*

7. *At the right, fold under the ends that extend beyond the pleats.*

8. *Open the pleats so the napkin stands up on the folds made in step 7.*

Wiesbaden

The Wiesbaden is a napkin fold that adorns many dining tables in the beautiful resort town of Wiesbaden, Germany. The fold, unique because it is anchored in the tines of a fork, looks best if made with a cloth or paper napkin no larger than 17 inches square. A larger napkin would be too heavy to be supported by a fork.

1

2

3

4

★★ Instructions

1. *Fold the napkin in half diagonally to form a triangle.*
2. *Place the folded edge at the bottom.*
3. *Fold up the bottom edge about one-and-one-half inches.*
4. *Accordian-pleat this shape into one-inch pleats. Anchor the bottom edge of the napkin by inserting it between the tines of a fork.*

Yesteryear

Beautiful table linens have always been admired and there are few, if any, times in history when they were not in great demand. When the Belgian city of Ypres was the center of the linen weaving trade in the sixteenth century, the demand for the beautiful fabric was so great that two sets of looms were made—large ones for weaving tablecloths and smaller ones for weaving napkins. By using looms of different sizes the fabric could be woven to the exact width desired.

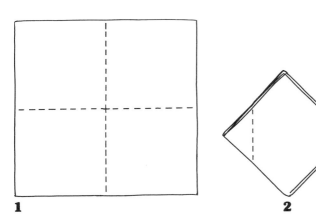

1   **2**   **3**   **4**

★★ Instructions

1. *Fold the napkin in quarters.*

2. *Place it so the free corners are at the top.*

3. *Fold the left and right corners to the center.*

4. *Turn the napkin over and accordian-pleat it into four equal pleats. Slip the napkin through a napkin ring or tie a ribbon around the center.*

Folds With
Two Napkins

Bouquet

The Bouquet requires two napkins of the same size but of contrasting color or design. Use one print and one solid or two different solid colors. Since both napkins must be pulled through a napkin ring, 17-inch-square napkins are best; folded with larger napkins, this shape becomes too bulky. The Bouquet can be folded with cloth or paper napkins.

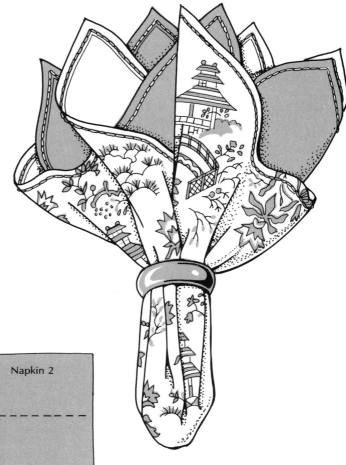

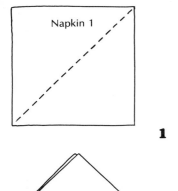

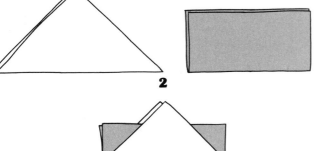

1

2

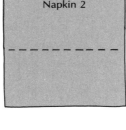

3

★★ Instructions

1. Fold one napkin in half diagonally to make a triangle. Fold the second one in half to make a rectangle.

2. Place the napkins so the folds are along the bottom edges.

3. Open the triangle and place the rectangle inside it. Hold the napkins together at the center of the bottom edge as you pull the bottom three inches through a napkin ring.

Double Fan

The Double Fan is an easy and quite versatile shape to fold. It can be made with two cloth napkins of contrasting colors, with one print and one solid, or with two paper napkins. If you choose cloth napkins, use the 17-inch-square size so the fan will not be too heavy to be supported by the glass. If using two paper napkins, the base may be inserted in a sturdy napkin ring.

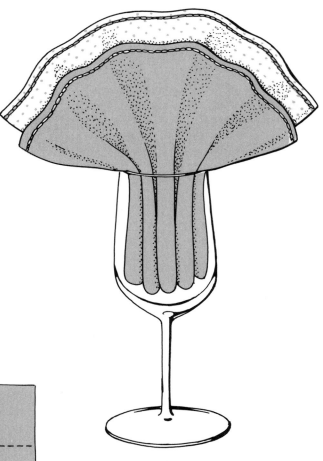

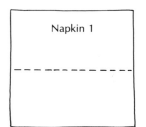

Napkin 1   Napkin 2

1

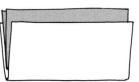

2

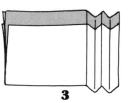

3

★ Instructions

1. *Fold each napkin in half to form a rectangle.*

2. *Place one napkin inside the other leaving about two to three inches of the inside napkin exposed.*

3. *Accordian-pleat the two napkins as if they were one, making the pleats about one inch wide. Place the bottom of the napkin in a glass and fan out the pleats.*

Mountain Laurel

The Mountain Laurel looks especially pretty if it is folded with two napkins of contrasting colors or with one floral print and one solid napkin. To make a matching napkin ring see page 122.

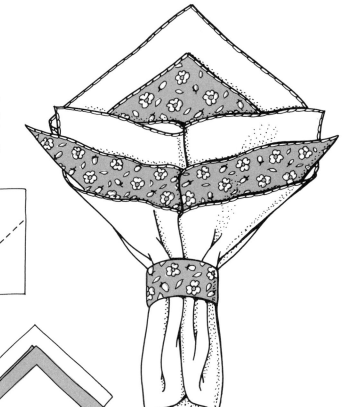

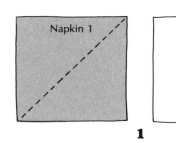

1

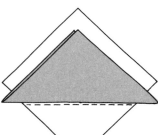

2

3

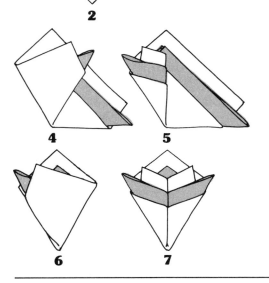

4   **5**

6   **7**

★★★ Instructions

1. *Fold one napkin in half diagonally to form a triangle. The second napkin will be folded diagonally also but with the bottom point about two inches lower than the top point.*

2. *Place the first napkin on top of the second napkin so the top point of the second is about one inch below the first.*

3. *Fold up the bottom of the first napkin.*

4. *Hold your finger at the center of the bottom edge as you fold the left side over, as shown.*

5. *Bring what was the left edge back so it is now even with the new left edge.*

6. *Bring the right edge over to the left edge.*

7. *Bring what was the right edge back so it is now even with the new right edge. Slip the bottom four inches through a napkin ring.*

Preening Peacock

César Ritz, founder of the elegant Ritz Hotel in Paris, spoke scornfully of the many elaborate napkin folds popular in the seventeenth and eighteenth centuries. Ritz favored simple shapes such as fans, palm leaves, boats, and roses. Although Ritz would have disapproved of it, the Preening Peacock enhances any dinner table. Instructions for the basic Peacock are on page 68.

1

fold

2

3

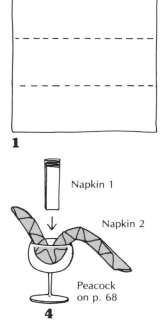

Napkin 1

Napkin 2

Peacock on p. 68

4

★★★★ Instructions

1. *Fold the napkin in thirds.*

2. *Place it so the fold is along the top edge.*

3. *Accordian-pleat the napkin into one-inch pleats.*

4. *Insert this shape into a glass with a Peacock in it (page 68). Let the pleats fan out.*

Swan

European style in the seventeenth century was highly ornamental. Dining tables of the well-to-do were usually set with a white linen cloth laid over a darker one, and napkins were folded in elaborate shapes such as animals, flowers, or decorative fans. The Swan would have been most appropriate in such a setting.

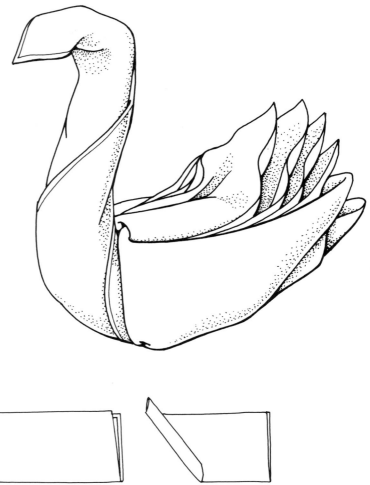

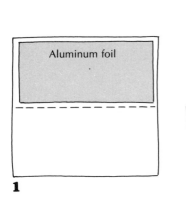

Aluminum foil

1

2

3

4

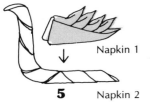

Bird-of-Paradise on p. 35

Napkin 1

5   Napkin 2

★★★★ Instructions

1. *Cut a piece of aluminum foil slightly smaller than one-half the size of the napkin. Place the napkin face down on the table and set the foil on the top half.*

2. *Fold the napkin in half covering the aluminum foil.*

3. *Starting at the lower left corner, begin to roll up the napkin.*

4. *Continue rolling until the napkin forms a long tube.*

5. *Bend half of the tube into an upright position and turn down the end to form the swan's head. Place a second napkin in the Bird-of-Paradise shape (page 35) on top of the flat portion of the tube so the corner points form the tail feathers of the swan.*

Children's Party Folds

Animal Faces

Three different Animal Faces can be made from small—12½- or 13½-inch-square—paper napkins. The first three steps for all the faces are the same, but subsequent steps are different, depending on which animal you choose. Use crayons or felt-tipped markers to draw the animal's distinctive features.

Brave Bull

Kindly Kitty

Regal Rabbit

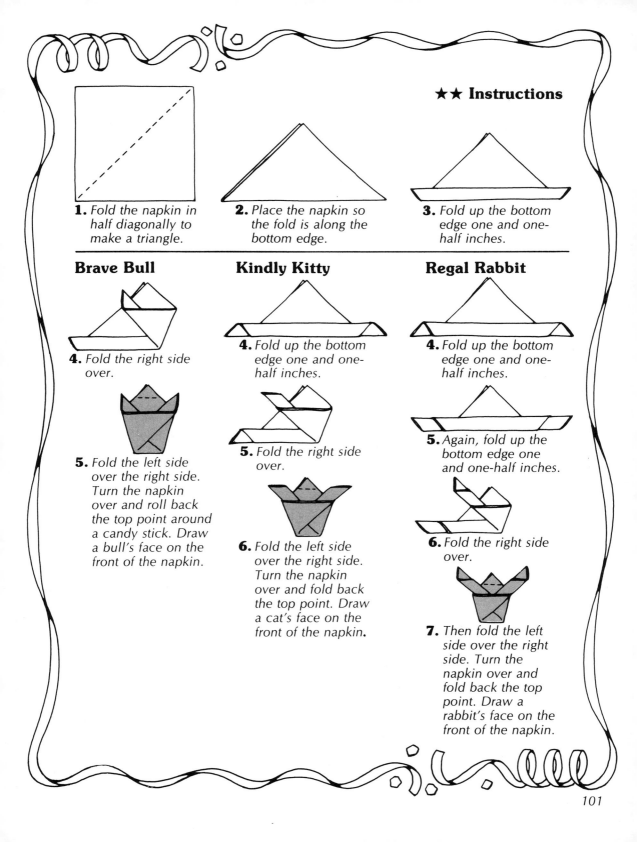

1. *Fold the napkin in half diagonally to make a triangle.*

2. *Place the napkin so the fold is along the bottom edge.*

3. *Fold up the bottom edge one and one-half inches.*

Brave Bull

4. *Fold the right side over.*

5. *Fold the left side over the right side. Turn the napkin over and roll back the top point around a candy stick. Draw a bull's face on the front of the napkin.*

Kindly Kitty

4. *Fold up the bottom edge one and one-half inches.*

5. *Fold the right side over.*

6. *Fold the left side over the right side. Turn the napkin over and fold back the top point. Draw a cat's face on the front of the napkin.*

Regal Rabbit

4. *Fold up the bottom edge one and one-half inches.*

5. *Again, fold up the bottom edge one and one-half inches.*

6. *Fold the right side over.*

7. *Then fold the left side over the right side. Turn the napkin over and fold back the top point. Draw a rabbit's face on the front of the napkin.*

Envelope Surprise

When folded as an Envelope Surprise, a small paper napkin (12½ or 13½ inches square) will hold a favor for a birthday party celebration. Wrapping the favors adds even more surprise.

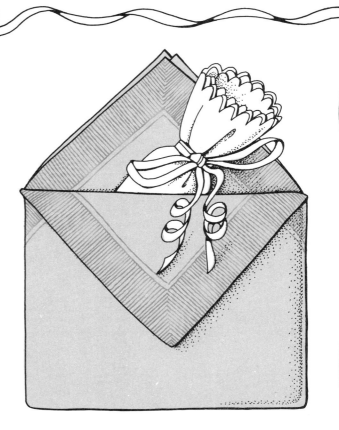

1

2

3

4   **5**

★★ Instructions

1. *Fold the napkin in quarters.*
2. *Place the napkin so the free corners are at the top.*
3. *Fold up the bottom point.*
4. *Fold in the right and left points.*
5. *Turn the napkin over and fold down the first layer of the top point.*

Kite

A Kite that looks just like the ones that glide through the sky can be made with a paper napkin. Use printed napkins or have children draw their own designs on plain ones.

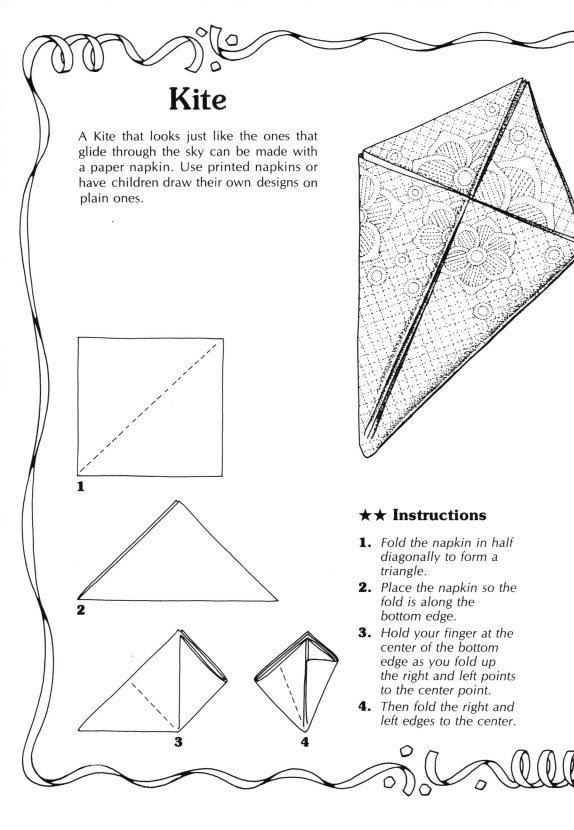

1

2

3   **4**

★★ Instructions

1. *Fold the napkin in half diagonally to form a triangle.*

2. *Place the napkin so the fold is along the bottom edge.*

3. *Hold your finger at the center of the bottom edge as you fold up the right and left points to the center point.*

4. *Then fold the right and left edges to the center.*

Name Tag

For a child's party, the Name Tag provides young guests with a very grown-up place card that lets them know where they are to sit. Write the names with a crayon or felt-tipped marker.

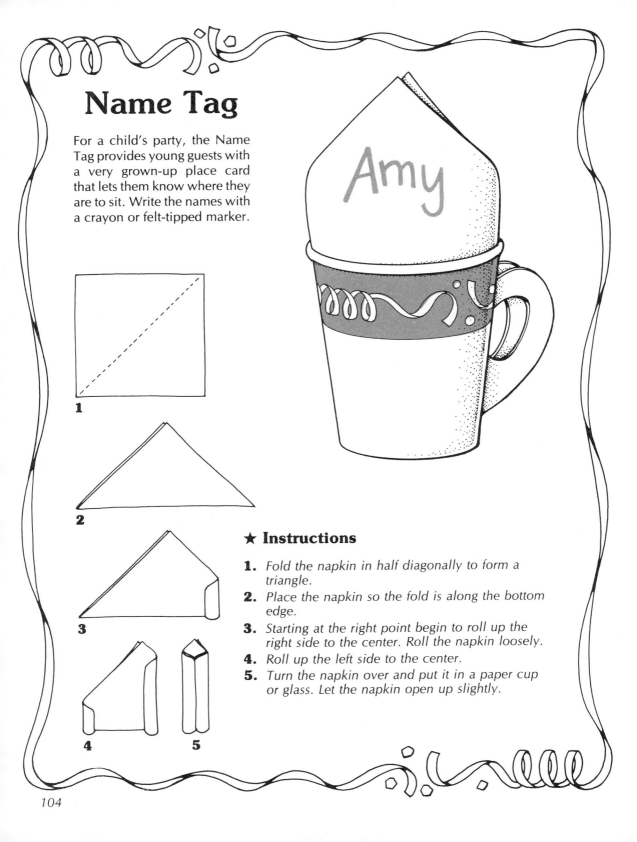

1

2

3

4   **5**

★ Instructions

1. *Fold the napkin in half diagonally to form a triangle.*

2. *Place the napkin so the fold is along the bottom edge.*

3. *Starting at the right point begin to roll up the right side to the center. Roll the napkin loosely.*

4. *Roll up the left side to the center.*

5. *Turn the napkin over and put it in a paper cup or glass. Let the napkin open up slightly.*

Paper Airplane

The Paper Airplane helps to create an aeronautical theme for a child's party. Be sure to have extra napkins on hand so the children can launch whole squadrons of planes if they wish—and they will.

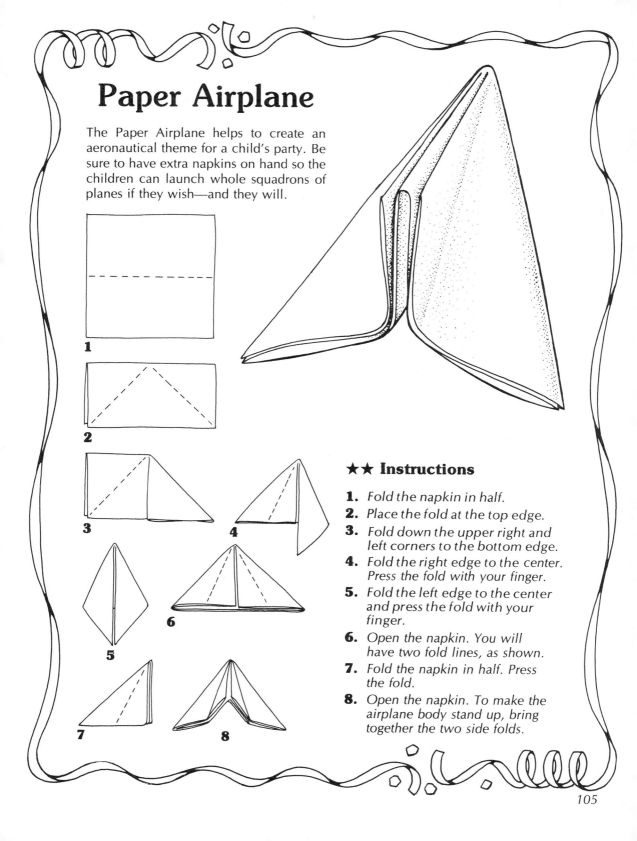

★★ Instructions

1. Fold the napkin in half.

2. Place the fold at the top edge.

3. Fold down the upper right and left corners to the bottom edge.

4. Fold the right edge to the center. Press the fold with your finger.

5. Fold the left edge to the center and press the fold with your finger.

6. Open the napkin. You will have two fold lines, as shown.

7. Fold the napkin in half. Press the fold.

8. Open the napkin. To make the airplane body stand up, bring together the two side folds.

Pinwheel

Children of all ages like the Pinwheel, a challenging fold that is well worth the effort.

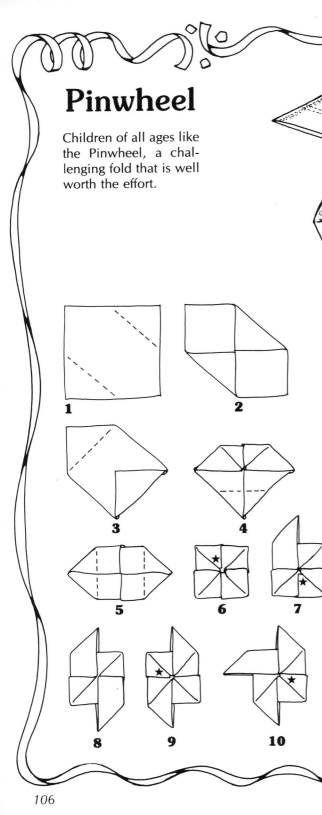

★★★★ Instructions

1. *Fold the upper right and lower left corners to the center.*
2. *The napkin will look like this.*
3. *Turn the napkin over and fold the lower right and upper left corners to the center. Turn the resulting square so one corner faces you.*
4. *Fold the top and bottom corners to the center.*
5. *Turn the napkin over and fold the left and right corners to the center.*
6. *Pull out the corner marked with a star in the drawing.*
7. *Now pull out the second corner marked with a star.*
8. *The napkin will look like this.*
9. *Turn the napkin over and pull out the corner marked with a star.*
10. *Pull out the last corner marked with a star.*

Royal Crown

The Royal Crown can be used as a party favor—just add stars (available at variety stores) and stripes (made with felt-tipped markers).

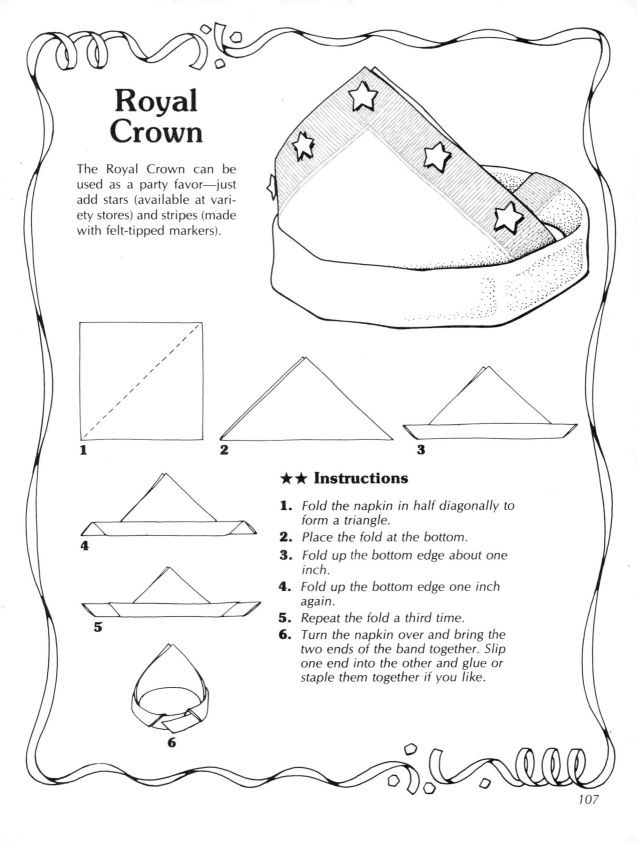

1

2

3

4

5

★★ Instructions

1. Fold the napkin in half diagonally to form a triangle.

2. Place the fold at the bottom.

3. Fold up the bottom edge about one inch.

4. Fold up the bottom edge one inch again.

5. Repeat the fold a third time.

6. Turn the napkin over and bring the two ends of the band together. Slip one end into the other and glue or staple them together if you like.

6

Sailboat

The Sailboat, a simple fold, lends a nautical air to a child's party. Folded in cloth, it makes a nice addition to a casual brunch, lunch, or supper table.

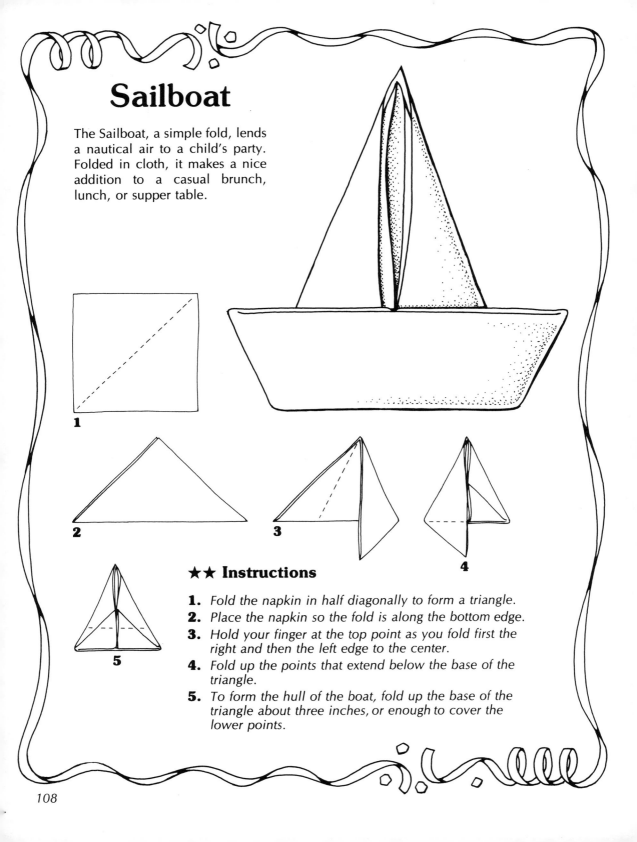

1

2

3

4

5

★★ Instructions

1. *Fold the napkin in half diagonally to form a triangle.*
2. *Place the napkin so the fold is along the bottom edge.*
3. *Hold your finger at the top point as you fold first the right and then the left edge to the center.*
4. *Fold up the points that extend below the base of the triangle.*
5. *To form the hull of the boat, fold up the base of the triangle about three inches, or enough to cover the lower points.*

Other
Table Accessories Made
With Napkins

Bottle Coaster

A Bottle Coaster will protect your table from the condensation that forms on a cold bottle of wine. It will also make it easier to handle the bottle when pouring. For the coaster, a cloth napkin 17 or 20 inches square is best. Napkins of cotton or linen are more absorbent than those made of synthetic fabrics.

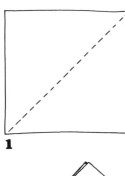

1

2

3

4

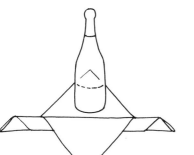

5

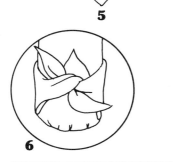

6

★★★ Instructions

1. *Fold the napkin in half diagonally to form a triangle.*

2. *Place the napkin so the fold is along the bottom edge.*

3. *Fold up the bottom edge one and one-half inches.*

4. *Once again, fold up the bottom edge one and one-half inches.*

5. *Fold down the top layer of the top point over the band at the bottom. Then place the bottle in the center of the top triangle.*

6. *Lift both triangles and the band against the bottle. Tie the ends of the band together at the back of the bottle making sure to catch the triangle at the back between the tie and the bottle.*

Vase Wrap

Potted plants make an attractive yet inexpensive centerpiece. For a grouping of three or more plants, try using flower pots of varying sizes. If the plants are arranged in a line, the pots can all be the same size. To wrap flower pots with napkins, choose those in colors that compliment the flowers as well as the color scheme of your table setting.

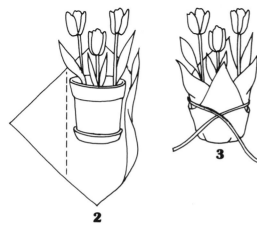

1

2

3

★★ Instructions

1. *Lay the napkin on the table and place the flower pot in the center.*
2. *Lift up two opposite corners; then lift up the two remaining corners.*
3. *Tie a length of ribbon or raffia around the flower pot to hold the corners of the napkin in place.*

Place Mat

To make a Place Mat for dinner plates, use a napkin that is at least 22 inches square. For luncheon or dessert plates, a 20-inch-square napkin is suitable. Choose napkins that harmonize with your china.

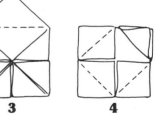

9" Dinner Plate

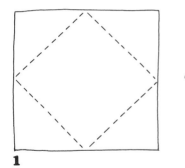

1

2

3

4

★★ Instructions

1. *Fold the corners of the napkin to the center.*
2. *The napkin will look like this.*
3. *Holding the center points in place, carefully turn the napkin over. Fold the corners to the center.*
4. *Carefully turn the napkin over. Pull each of the center points to the outside corners. Give each one a slight tug so the point will lie flat on the table.*

Napkin Trivet

A Trivet that protects a table from hot dishes can be made with two napkins, one for the base and one for the decorative top. The base is folded like the Place Mat (opposite); the top is made by following the directions given below.

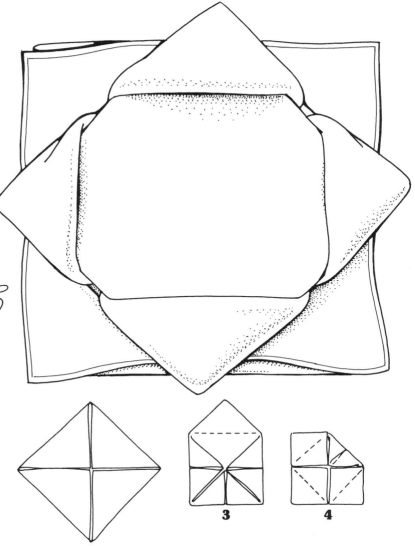

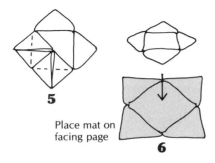

1

2

3

4

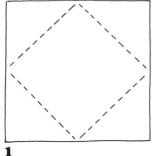

5

Place mat on
facing page

6

★★★★ Instructions

1. Fold the corners of the napkin to the center.

2. The napkin will look like this.

3. Turn the napkin over and again fold the corners to the center.

4. Turn the napkin over and again fold the corners to the center.

5. Turn the napkin over and pull the center points to the outside corners.

6. Place this fold on top of a napkin folded in the shape of a Place Mat (opposite).

Bread Basket

To make a Bread Basket you will need three matching napkins at least 20 inches square. Traditionally called a gondola, this fold can hold rolls or bread or hot loaf dishes encased in pastry.

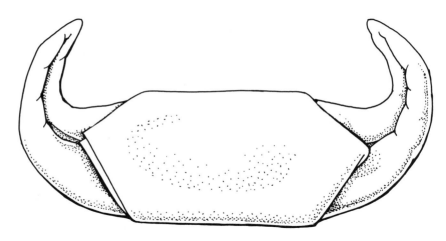

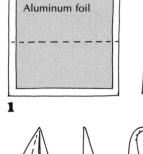

1

2

3

4

5   **6**   fold   **7**

Napkin 1   Napkin 2

8

9

Napkin 3

10   **11**

★★★★ Instructions

1. *Place a piece of aluminum foil slightly smaller than the napkin in the center of the napkin.*
2. *Fold the napkin in half so the aluminum foil is on the inside.*
3. *Fold top corners to bottom edge.*
4. *Fold both edges to the center.*
5. *Again, fold the right and left edges to the center.*
6. *Fold the napkin in half.*
7. *Bend the top point into a curve.*
8. *Repeat steps 1 through 7 with a second napkin. Place the two napkins on a plate.*
9. *Fold the third napkin in quarters.*
10. *Place free points at the top.*
11. *Fold the right and left corners to the center. Place this napkin on top of the other two.*

How To Make
Your Own
Table Accessories

Making Fabric Napkins

To create napkins in a fabric that coordinates with your table accessories, all you need is the fabric and a little stitching know-how.

Linen, cotton, polyester, or a blend of any two of these are appropriate for making napkins. The fabrics are available in a variety of weights from sheer to coarse, but for most folds a medium weight is best.

The type of finished edge used is dictated to some extent by the fabric chosen. Linen napkins are usually finished with a hand-rolled hem, a machine-stitched edge, or a mitered hem. More casual cotton and polyester fabrics may have decorative borders of embroidery, lace, or a contrasting binding. If you prefer a fringed edge, select a coarse fabric to give the fringe some weight.

The instructions that follow are for 20-inch-square napkins. To make a set of eight, you will need 2½ yards of 45-inch-wide fabric. For a special border, you will need 2⅜ yards of edging for each napkin or 20 yards for eight. Choose the type of edge you want from among the seven described below. Before cutting the fabric, read the instructions. Different finishing techniques require varying hem allowances.

Blanket stitch:
Cut a 21-inch square of fabric. Press a ¼-inch doubled hem around the edges. Secure thread on the underside. Insert needle from top about ¼ inch above left edge, keeping thread from previous stitch under point of needle. Repeat around the edges.

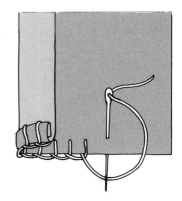

Hand-rolled hems
1. Cut a 21-inch square of fabric. Machine-stitch slightly more than ¼ inch inside edges. Trim fabric outside stitching.
2. Fold fabric along stitch line making sure stitches do not show on right side. Working from right to left, take a small stitch through top layer of fold. Pick up a few threads of fabric below the stitch. Make several stitches then pull thread to roll hem. Miter the ends (below), or make a square corner (opposite, top).

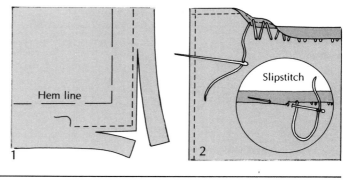

Hem line

Slipstitch

Mitered corners
1. Cut a 21-inch square of fabric. Trim off corner diagonally leaving a ¼-inch margin at corner point. Fold over the margin.
2. Press a ¼-inch doubled hem along the sides. Slipstitch the folded edges to the napkin.
3. At the corners, the folded edges will meet to form a miter. Slipstitch together the mitered edges along the diagonal line.

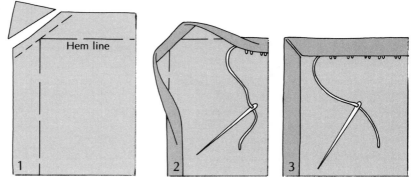

Hem line

Machine-stitched hems

1. Cut a 21-inch square of fabric. Press a ¼-inch doubled hem around the edges. Unfold all but one side. Machine-stitch the folded hem from end to end as close as possible to the inside fold.

2. Turn under the adjacent side and stitch in a similar fashion to form a square corner. Repeat the procedure on the remaining two sides.

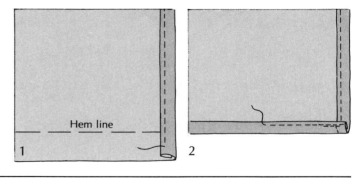

Fringed edges

1. For a 20-inch napkin with ½-inch-long fringe, cut a 21-inch square of fabric. Pin-baste a line ½ inch from the edge. Starting with the outermost thread, gently pull out the crosswise threads that lie outside the line of pins. Repeat along the remaining edges. Remove the pins.

2. To prevent unraveling, machine-stitch just inside the fringe around all four edges.

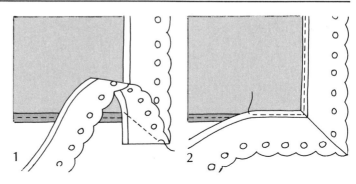

Lace trim

1. Cut a 20½-inch square of fabric. Press up a ¼-inch hem on all four edges and machine stitch along the fold. On one side, pin the straight edge of the lace on top of the hem and stitch through the hem from corner to corner. Extend the lace past the edge of the napkin, then fold it back on itself. Stitch a diagonal line from corner of the napkin to corner of the lace.

2. Align lace along adjacent edge and attach as before, making a diagonal line of stitching through lace at each corner.

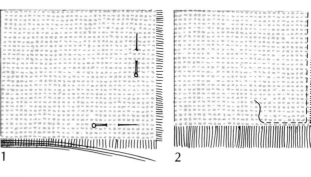

Double-fold bias binding

1. Cut a 20-inch square of fabric. Slip binding over one edge of fabric and machine stitch catching both top and bottom edges of the binding.

2. Pin binding along adjacent edge, folding in excess at the corner to form a diagonal fold.

3. Insert needle at the inner end of fold; stitch and back stitch to secure it. Then stitch next side, repeating procedure to bind corner.

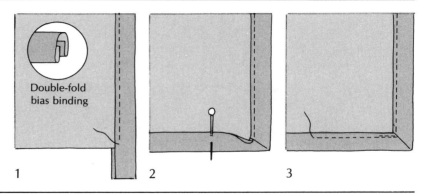

Embroidering Initials

The classic way of personalizing a napkin is with elegant initials. For best results, use the slanted satin stitch illustrated at right. It is a solid stitch that covers an initial with long, slanted lines. Place the letter diagonally at one corner of the napkin, as shown below, or straight at the bottom of the right corner. To trace the initials from these pages or other sources, you will need tracing paper, a black felt-tipped marker, and a dressmaker's pencil. For stitching you will need six-strand embroidery thread and a crewel needle. Use only two strands of the thread.

To transfer an initial onto a napkin, cover the letter with tracing paper, and, with a black felt-tipped marker, trace its outline on the paper. Place the appropriate corner of the napkin over the initial; the initial should show through the fabric. With a dressmaker's pencil, trace the outline of the initial on the fabric.

1. To make a slanted satin stitch, start in center of the initial to establish angle of slant. Bring needle up from wrong side of fabric at lower edge of traced outline. Insert needle in upper line of tracing slightly to the right of where thread entered fabric. Bring it out again to the right of previous stitch.

2. Continue in this manner, following the shape of the letter as you stitch and working from left to right. Place the stitches close together and maintain an even tension.

3. At the narrow ends, keep the stitches slanted but make them increasingly smaller to fit within the tracing.

The alphabet on these pages is drawn with the letters filled in to make tracing around them easier. As illustrated above, trace only the outline of a letter on the napkin. The stitches will fill in the space between lines.

A B

C D E F

Decorating Fabric Napkins

Personalized napkins can be a conversation piece, especially if the decoration you choose for the napkins matches your china, a favorite tablecloth, or the dining room wallpaper. The design may also tie in with a particular occasion: a trefoil for St. Patrick's Day, fireworks for the Fourth of July, flowers for the arrival of spring, or suits of cards for a bridge party. You can even make children more aware of table manners if you let them decorate their own napkins.

The first step in decorating a napkin is to choose a design, the source of which might be anywhere. The design of a ceramic tile or even a package label may be inspiring. Or an idea might come from a favorite scarf, a piece of jewelry, or your kitchen curtains. Look at magazines and newspapers for interesting uses of letters to create monograms. Children's toys, coloring books, and story books are full of illustrations that would make wonderful decorations for napkins. Simply look around you and you will find hundreds of ideas to adapt.

Once chosen, a design or motif will probably have to be enlarged or reduced to fit the napkin. (Follow the instructions below). The design may be placed at the bottom right corner of the napkin or it may be centered diagonally in one corner, or, if large, it may cover the entire napkin. A decorative border looks best if made completely around all four sides.

Napkins can be decorated in a variety of ways. For special fabric paints and fabric dyes, you will need mixing jars, paintbrushes, tailor's chalk, masking tape, and newspapers

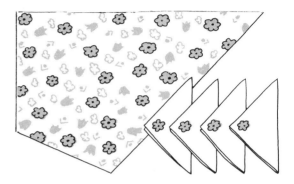

to cover your work area. Fabric markers and transfer crayons are even easier to use. Read the directions that accompany the craft material you have chosen to see what type of fabric is suitable. Some methods require natural fabrics, others work best on synthetics. Also make sure that the care requirements of the fabric and the coloring material you are using are identical.

Enlarging and Reducing a Design

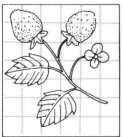

Original size

To change the size of a design, first trace it onto a square piece of paper. Fold the paper into quarters twice; unfold it. The paper will now be marked by fold lines into 16 equal boxes.

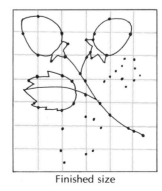

Finished size

Now cut a piece of paper into a square equal to the finished size of your design (either larger or smaller than the original). Fold the paper into quarters twice; unfold it. The paper will now be marked by fold lines into 16 equal boxes. Copy the design from the first square to the second, box by box.

Fabric paints and fabric markers, available in craft shops or art supply stores, are the fastest means of decorating napkins. To paint a design freehand, secure the napkin to your work surface with masking tape and draw the outline of the design with tailor's chalk. Apply one color and allow it to dry before adding the next so the colors do not run together.

To make a crayon transfer, draw your design in reverse on paper. Then place the crayoned side face down on top of the napkin and iron the design following the crayon manufacturer's directions for time and proper temperature. This method is especially fun for children.

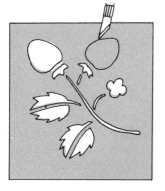

(Writing their names backwards can be a real challenge.)

A simple design to create with fabric dyes requires only two or three colors, bowls, and some napkins. Mix the dyes according to the package directions, putting each color in a separate shallow bowl. Fold the napkins many times until you have a small square. Dip one corner or one edge of the napkin into a bowl

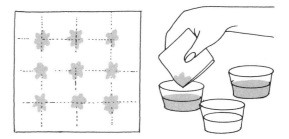

of dye for a few seconds, or until it absorbs some color. Repeat, using different sides or corners and varying the colors of dye. Carefully unfold the napkin and lay it flat to dry; each napkin will have a slightly different design.

Paper napkins can be decorated with crayons or felt-tipped markers, and they will add a festive note to even a simple soup-and-sandwich lunch. Children will enjoy setting the table if it includes napkins of their own design.

Making and Using a Stencil

To make a stencil, draw a design in pencil on heavy stencil paper. With masking tape, secure paper to the top of some newspapers. With a craft knife, carefully cut out each area of the design to be painted, making sure to leave connecting "islands" between the open areas.

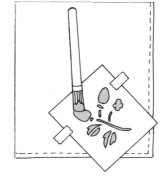

To stencil a napkin, first tape it to a work surface, then tape stencil on top. With a blunt, stiff stencil brush, dab paint over cut-out areas; do not overload brush. For two or more colors, cover with paper areas to be painted in other colors. Let each color dry before applying another or removing the stencil.

Making Napkin Rings

Nothing is more becoming to certain napkin folds than a beautiful napkin ring, and, as you see on these pages, rings can be made from materials you have on hand—paper towel tubes, fabric, flour, and flower blossoms. Another way of creating napkin rings is to use your favorite craft or hobby. For example, make a 5- to 6-inch-long macramé or crochet chain. Tie the ends together and trim off the excess to finish the ring. Or make a braid of ¼-inch-wide ribbon and finish it the same way. Small shells collected at the beach can be drilled with a hole and threaded with a 5-inch-long strand of elastic. Children will enjoy drawing pictures on a 3-by-6-inch strip of paper that can be glued to form a napkin ring. As you can see, the range of ideas for napkin rings is limited only by your imagination.

Bread Dough Napkin Rings: Inedible bread dough can be sculpted into rings.

Recipe
4 cups all-purpose flour
1 cup salt
1½ cups water

Combine ingredients. Place dough on a pastry board and knead for 8 minutes; if it is too stiff, add a little water. Shape dough with your hands or roll into a ½-inch-thick slab with a rolling pin. Make pattern, place it on slab, trace around it, and cut out the shape with a knife. Bake on aluminum foil-covered cooky sheet for 1½ hours at 325° F. Bake until golden brown or remove from oven while still white and decorate with acrylic paints. Apply polyurethane to preserve the rings.

Fabric-Covered Napkin Ring: For eight rings, you will need one paper-towel tube, a 6-by-20-inch piece of fabric, a pencil, scissors, and white glue. Measure and mark 1¼-inch intervals along the tube and cut through the tube at each mark. Cut fabric into eight 6-by-2½-inch strips.

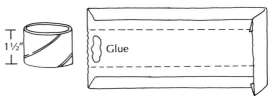

Press a ¼-inch hem on long sides. Apply glue to short end.

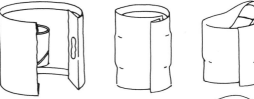

Starting with glued end, wrap fabric around tube. Glue opposite end and secure it to tube. Glue inside of tube; fold top and bottom fabric edges to inside of tube and press them against the sides.

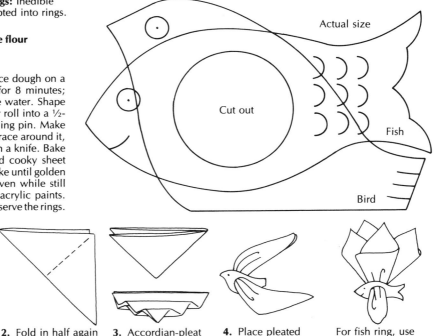

Actual size

Cut out

Fish

Bird

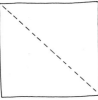 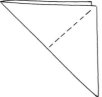

1. Fold napkin in half to make a triangle.

2. Fold in half again for smaller triangle.

3. Accordian-pleat the triangle.

4. Place pleated shape in bird ring.

For fish ring, use Nosegay (page 24).

Daisy Chain: Any hardy fresh flower with small blossoms can be braided into a chain to form a napkin ring. You will need: one yard narrow ribbon per ring, flower blossoms with at least 2-inch-long stems (the number will vary with their size), and scissors.

1. Cut ribbon into three 12-inch-long strands. Tie them together about 2 inches in from one end. Place first flower blossom near the knot with its stem lying along the right-hand strand of ribbon.

2. To begin braiding, bring right strand over center strand, treating stem and right strand as one.

3. Now bring left strand over center strand. Continue braiding, alternating right and then left strand over center one until flower stem is secured.

4. Add next flower when another strand is in right position. Braid until stem is secure. Then add next flower and continue braiding. When chain is 5 inches long, knot working end to starting end and trim off excess.

Felt Blossom: This napkin ring is made of four pieces of felt: one leaf, two petal layers, and a ring whose ends form the innermost petals. You will need: a 6-by-7-inch piece of felt for petals and a 6-inch-square of green felt for the leaf of each blossom, tracing paper, cardboard, pencil, scissors. Trace and cut out each shape separately so you have four patterns. Then trace those shapes onto cardboard and cut them out. Now trace and cut out the shapes in felt. Cut a ⅝-inch slit in center of petals and leaf. Align slits and insert ends of ring from below.

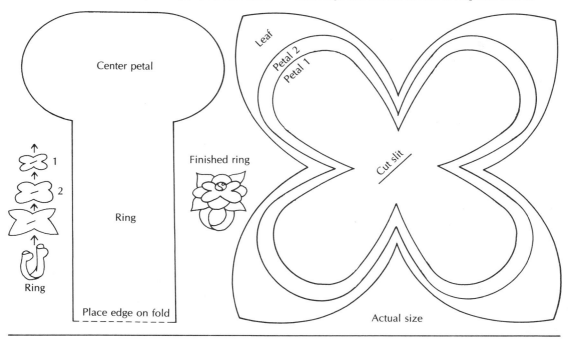

Index of Folds

Fold	Page	Flat	Standing	Cloth	Paper	13-inch	17-inch	20-inch	Complexity
Ahoy	30		x	x	x		x	x	★★
Algonquin	31	x		x			x	x	★★★
Animal Faces	100	x			x	x			★★
Arrowhead	32		x	x				x	★★★
Artichoke	33	x		x			x	x	★★★★
Astarte	34		x	x				x	★★★★
Astoria	18	x		x	x		x	x	★ QUICK
Bird-of-Paradise	35		x	x				x	★★★★
Bishop's Hat	36		x	x	x		x	x	★★★
Bouquet	94	x		x	x		x		★★
Bottle Coaster	110		x	x			x	x	★★★
Bow Tie	19	x		x			x	x	★ QUICK
Bread Basket	114		x	x				x	★★★★
Buffet Servers	38	x		x	x		x	x	★
Candle	40		x	x	x		x	x	★★
Cathedral	41	x		x			x	x	★★
Chloe	20	x		x	x	x	x	x	★ QUICK
Crown	42		x	x	x		x	x	★★★
Davallia	43	x		x	x		x	x	★

Fold	Page	Flat	Standing	Cloth	Paper	13-inch	17-inch	20-inch	Complexity
Debevoise	21	x		x	x	x	x	x	★ QUICK
Diamond	44	x		x				x	★★★★
Double Bill	45	x		x			x	x	★★
Double Fan	95		x	x	x	x	x	x	★
Echeverria	46	x	x	x			x	x	★★
Echo	47	x		x			x	x	★★★
Elegante	48	x		x	x		x	x	★★
Emerald	49	x		x			x	x	★★
Envelope Surprise	102	x		x	x	x	x	x	★★
Erin	50		x	x	x	x	x	x	★★
Fan	22		x	x	x	x	x	x	★ QUICK
Flamingo	51	x		x	x		x	x	★★
Fleur-de-lis	52		x	x	x		x	x	★★★
Flower Basket	53	x		x	x		x	x	★★★
Flower Pot	54	x		x			x	x	★★★
Fortunella	55	x		x	x		x	x	★
Hyacinth	56		x	x			x	x	★★★
Iris	57	x		x			x	x	★★★

Fold	Page	Flat	Standing	Cloth	Paper	13-inch	17-inch	20-inch	Complexity
Irish Ripples	58	x		x			x	x	★★★
Kite	103	x		x	x	x	x	x	★★
Lily	59		x	x			x	x	★★
Luncheon	23	x		x	x		x	x	★ QUICK
Mexican Fan	60		x	x	x		x	x	★★★
Monogram	61	x		x			x	x	★★★
Mountain Laurel	96	x		x	x		x	x	★★★
Name Tag	104		x		x	x	x		★
Napkin Trivet	113	x		x				x	★★★★
New Square	62	x		x			x	x	★★
Nosegay	24	x		x	x		x	x	★ QUICK
Obelisk	63		x	x	x		x	x	★★
Orchid	64	x		x			x	x	★★★
Palm Frond	65		x	x				x	★
Paper Airplane	105	x		x	x	x	x		★★
Party Hat	66		x	x				x	★★

Fold	Page	Flat	Standing	Cloth	Paper	13-inch	17-inch	20-inch	Complexity
Party Wheel	67	x		x	x		x	x	★★
Peacock	68		x	x	x		x	x	★★★
Peony	69		x	x			x	x	★★★
Philodendron	70	x		x			x	x	★
Phoenix	71	x		x				x	★★★
Pierre	25	x		x			x	x	★ QUICK
Pineapple	72		x	x			x	x	★★★
Pinwheel	106	x			x	x	x		★★★
Place Mat	112	x		x				x	★★
Poinsettia	73		x	x				x	★★★★
Preening Peacock	97		x	x	x		x	x	★★★★
Pyramid	74		x	x				x	★★★
Queen Anne	75		x	x			x	x	★★★
Reflections	76	x		x	x		x	x	★★★
Regimental Stripe	77	x		x			x	x	★★
Rio	78	x		x			x	x	★★
Roll	26	x		x			x	x	★ QUICK
Rose	79	x		x				x	★★★★
Royal Crown	107		x		x	x			★★
Rugby	80	x		x	x		x	x	★★

Fold	Page	Flat	Standing	Cloth	Paper	13-inch	17-inch	20-inch	Complexity
Sailboat	108	x		x	x	x	x	x	★★
Sapphire	81	x		x				x	★★★★
Soave	27		x	x	x		x	x	★ QUICK
Sphinx	28		x	x	x		x	x	★ QUICK
Swan	98		x	x				x	★★★★
Swedish Bayonets	82		x	x				x	★★★★
Tavern	83		x	x	x		x	x	★★
Temple Bells	84		x	x				x	★★★★
Traditional Folds	10	x		x	x	x	x	x	★
Tulip	85		x	x				x	★★★★
Van Dyke	86	x		x	x	x	x	x	★★
Vase Wrap	111		x	x	x	x	x	x	★★
Victoria	87	x		x			x	x	★★
Water Lily	88		x	x	x		x	x	★★★
Wedding Ring	89	x		x			x	x	★★★★
Wendy's Fan	90		x	x				x	★★★★
Wiesbaden	91		x	x	x	x	x		★★
Yesteryear	92	x		x			x	x	★★